Vaudeville's Wildflower

Vaudeville's Wildflower

The Many Lives of Cora Youngblood Corson

JAMES P. GREGORY JR.

LOUISIANA STATE UNIVERSITY PRESS ✾ BATON ROUGE

Published by Louisiana State University Press
lsupress.org

LSU Press Paperback Original
Designer: Kaelin Chappell Broaddus
Typefaces: Corundum Text Book, text; Cantoria MT Std, Ephemera Kingsford, WTR Roycroft, display

The manufacturer's authorized representative in the EU for product safety is Mare Nostrum Group B.V., Doelen 72, 4831 GR Breda, The Netherlands. Email: gpsr@mare-nostrum.co.uk.

Cover photograph: "Stage actress Cora Youngblood Corson," University of Washington Libraries, Special Collections, JWS16004.

Portions of the introduction first appeared in James P. Gregory Jr., "The Story of Cora Youngblood Corson," *ITEA Journal* 48, no. 4 (2021): 66–75.

Cataloging-in-Publication Data are available from the Library of Congress.

ISBN 978-0-8071-8677-0 (pbk.: alk. paper) —
ISBN 978-0-8071-8716-6 (pdf) — ISBN 978-0-8071-8715-9 (epub)

To the countless women whose artistry
was lost between the lines of history.
This work is a small act of remembrance,
a way to let your music play on.

CONTENTS

ILLUSTRATIONS

ACKNOWLEDGMENTS

My work on the life of Cora Youngblood Corson has been a difficult path to research for many reasons. Not only was it outside of my comfort area of research but also there are no collections on which to base my research. Therefore, the first start came from tracking down family members to see if they had any photos or documents related to Cora. For this, I owe thanks to my mother, Michelle Kagebein, for being the first to share the genealogy wherein I discovered Cora. I also owe a lot of thanks to Dale Ingram for his friendship and willingness to discuss writing styles and sources as we created works on a similar path. From here, I owe many thanks to those in my extended family and friends who helped me gather the photos, trunks, and documents. Thank you, Rebecca Nally, Johanne Geraldine Youngblood Crittenden, Linda Mitchell, Kelli Youngblood, Don Harry, Michael Lynch, Kevin Mungons, David Earll, Michael Corson, Patti and Allan Horst, Iris and Rick Schwartz, Michael Brubaker, Jill Stinnett, John Maestri, Brennan Gauthier, Kyle Davenport, and many others who have helped me over the years.

In getting this story out to the public, I also owe thanks to several academics who aided me in getting an article published. I am indebted to Douglas Yeo for guiding my writing. I am also grateful to Dr. Gail Robertson for bringing me into this realm of research, encouraging my work, and connecting me with such a wide variety of historians and musicians who have helped me tremendously. I also owe a great many thanks to Joanna Hersey for giving me opportunities to share my work on Cora and for connecting me to other historians who offered their help in my research. I also owe great thanks to Dr. Mark Janzen for his assistance in editing this work and for his mentorship over the years. Thank you to my dissertation committee for their guidance: Dr. Warren Metcalf, Dr. Cori Simon, Dr. Jennifer Holland, and Dr. Matt Stock.

Finally, I owe thanks to the women of the International Women's Brass Conference, who saw fit to award Cora the Pioneer Award for her work. I would also like to thank my wife, Stephanie, for supporting me throughout this project and listening to me talk about Cora far too much. If I left anyone out, I sincerely apologize and thank you for your assistance.

Vaudeville's Wildflower

INTRODUCTION

Understanding Cora's Life

I was born in Ada, Oklahoma, which sits in the Chickasaw Nation. At the age of three, I attended school as a part of the Chickasaw Nation Preschool and Head Start Program. A few years later, in elementary school in Collinsville, Oklahoma, which sits north of Tulsa in the Cherokee Nation, I attended Cherokee language and culture courses after school. I have reflected on my early education and wondered why I took part in these programs, since I am not an enrolled citizen of any tribe. I never questioned it, growing up. My family always told me that I was part Native American and that was enough for me to proudly announce this fact throughout my early years. Now, with the advances in DNA testing and my ability to research genealogy, I have discovered that I have no Native heritage at all. I wondered why my family had been so comfortable in perpetuating this incorrect assertion of our identity. This question led me on a journey through my family tree, gathering oral histories, scrapbooks, photo albums, and trunks of material to discover where this misconception came from.

When I asked my parents, I received a typical Oklahoma answer: "Your great-grandmother was a Cherokee princess!" Further prodding revealed that my father believed we were Native because his grandmother's last name was

Youngblood, she came from Anadarko, Oklahoma, which had been Kiowa, Comanche, and Apache lands, and she received "oil checks" for the entirety of her life. This gave me a jump-off point to begin my research, and it eventually led me to a portrait of "Princess Youngblood," in full Native regalia, taken in New York City in 1928. My family's "princess" was Cora Youngblood Corson, the sister of my great-great-grandfather.

This opened a world of questions for me: Who was she? Why was she being portrayed as Princess Youngblood? Was she Native American? When I began to dig into the question, I found a woman who took the country by storm in the 1910s as one of the greatest musicians of her time. She sold out hundreds of theaters, broke major performance records, led union strikes, braved submarines and air raids during World War I, performed for four presidents, and did this all as a woman trying to find her position in a field dominated by male musicians.

For several decades in the early twentieth century, nobody had to ask "Who is Cora Youngblood Corson?" Her name regularly appeared in newspapers around the country, and she was a fixture on the concert stage and vaudeville circuit. As a euphonium and tuba player, she was praised as being one of the greats of her time. She played for presidents, a woman of high class who became independently wealthy and moved in the rarified world of celebrities, and her endorsements drove sales of musical instruments. Yet despite her fame, she died in relative obscurity. Her complex life involved playing not only euphonium and tuba but also trombone, cello, and bagpipes, and included union activism, farming, and an eyebrow-raising lifetime of cultural appropriation, but she remains little understood. Today, even her family does not fully understand the trails she blazed, the battles she fought to accomplish her goals, and the important legacy she left behind.

I am twice related to Cora Youngblood Corson and Her Sextette. My great-great-grandfather Isaac Youngblood was Cora's brother. He married Mae McBride, who played the trombone with Cora's famous sextet. Four generations later, I began a doctoral research project in history at the University of Oklahoma, researching Cora after I saw her name and photographs in a family genealogy book.

I do not claim to be a musician, though I played trombone and euphonium through middle and high school. As a military historian who focuses on personal perspectives and the intermingling of culture with war efforts, I entered

Cora's life through her work with the Knights of Columbus during World War I, when she played for Allied troops in the United Kingdom, France, and Germany. Yet as I began to unpack her story, it quickly became clear that learning more about Cora would not be a straight path. She has largely been forgotten in history books; there are no archives or museums that have preserved her memory. Her legacy began to unfold as I asked more questions, and I learned that Cora's family—my family—had a great deal of material hiding in plain sight that spoke of her life and work. Distant relatives I had never met gave me scrapbooks, photographs, trunks of clothing, and documents that illuminated Cora's life. Families of those whom Cora touched also kept treasures and graciously donated them to me, all in the hope that Cora's story would be told. As the layers of her life began to reveal themselves, I realized just how significant a role she had played in many facets of history. Not only that, but I also learned that much of the information about her that has appeared in diverse media over the course of more than one hundred years is inaccurate. In fact, Cora Youngblood Corson had not one but many stories, as she projected many aspects of her personality in different ways.

One of the stories follows why she performed as a Native American through several points of her career. It is an important piece that we must discuss in some detail, but if you would like a deeper discussion of her ethnic impersonation, please see my dissertation, "The Performance of Self: The Story of Cora Youngblood Corson," available through the University of Oklahoma. Performing in full tribal regalia as a Native American, Cora subverted cultural stereotypes by portraying Natives as modern entertainers rather than as people of the past. Her musical ability astounded her contemporaries, who were shocked to see a Native *and* a woman outperform white men on the tuba and euphonium. Crowds flocked to theaters to see this Native woman who grew up on the plains of Oklahoma perform "Indian songs," opera, and jazz with skill unmatched by any other. Later in her career, she joined the all-Native Indian Reservation Band and performed for Presidents Herbert Hoover, Calvin Coolidge, and Franklin D. Roosevelt.

Surprisingly, however, she has no Native heritage. Throughout her career, Cora continually reinvented herself by manipulating racial, national, and class representations to remain unique in vaudeville. Today, we acknowledge these white performers as "ethnic impersonators" who used Native personas to present themselves on stage. Cora operated in the public eye during the period in which Native performers became more common in popular culture. Thanks to her observational knowledge of Natives in Oklahoma, Cora passed as a Native American, which allowed her to weave through a male-dominated world and draw support for her career and personal causes.

Cora's ability came from her time spent in Oklahoma, which enabled her to draw upon her knowledge of Native people she had lived alongside and imitate it for her audience when needed. Oklahoma is, and has been, a melting pot of many cultures, home to many blended communities of various ethnic backgrounds. In the early twentieth century, Oklahoma became a state, and celebrities from the state created the cultural image of those who claim to be Oklahoman, such as Cora Youngblood Corson. Their reputations and representations reflected the reputation of the state and created the image and culture of Oklahoma for a national audience.

In the late 1800s, the image produced by the popularity of westerns and dime novels created a certain image of Native Americans based around the Plains tribes. Novels achieved new levels of fame, including Karl May's *Winnetou,* which became a bestseller that told of wondrous adventures in the American West. Alongside the novels, Wild West shows and circuses like Buffalo Bill's Wild West Show capitalized on the popularity and drew heavily on a stereotyped Plains tribal image, thrilling audiences with living representations of their favorite novels. Native performers would dress in stereotypical headdresses and buckskins and ride around on horseback in front of rapt audiences. Artists such as Frederic Remington also instilled his popular sculptures, engravings, and paintings with this image.[1] The American public became convinced that "authentic" Native culture included eagle feather headbands, beads, and war whoops.

This new perception of what a Native American was, and the popularity of Native imagery in the early 1900s, led to a rapid increase in white Americans donning costumes and presenting themselves as Native. The reasoning for this varies, ranging from a desire for fame, popularity, land possession, or an escape from social constraints of the time. Playing Indian is, as Philip Deloria argues, "a persistent tradition in American culture."[2]

For most Americans in the early 1900s, "except in certain regions of the West and Southwest, living natives were visible to non-Indians mainly as performers: feathered and painted 'savages' in the immensely popular Wild West shows, picturesque figures in the landscape presented to tourists by enterprising companies in the Southwest and in the Great Lakes region, 'primitives' on display at world's fairs such as those in Chicago, Omaha, and St. Louis."[3] This popularity drew to vaudeville crowds that wanted to see their imagination made manifest on stage. Native performers used this to their advantage, to build careers and present to the public a new image of Native Americans. Alongside these Indigenous performers, however, non-Indian ethnic impersonators also took advantage of the popularity of Natives to advance their own careers.

Cora Youngblood Corson followed this path by adopting a Native persona, joining a growing number of white individuals in the early twentieth century, such as Archie Belaney, an Englishman who became known as Grey Owl, or Sylvester Long, known as Chief Buffalo Child Long Lance. This phenomenon was common, and for Cora the idea of using a Native persona eventually evolved into actively announcing that she was of Cherokee descent. She did this to reinvent herself in a field where not evolving equated with the end of a career.

Of course, this idea of stereotypes becoming the defining image of a monolithic "Indian" people is cause for debate, especially in discussions of cultural appropriation, because there is no consensus. Modern arguments point to the stereotypes as harmful representations, while others argue that the popularity they offered provided a way to reappropriate the imagery. In vaudeville and subsequent forms of entertainment, Native performers also graced the stage and performed stereotypical "Indian songs" in buckskin outfits adorned with beads and feathers. For instance, the Muscogee singer Tsianina Redfeather Blackstone, or "Princess Tsianina," performed around the world in vaudeville, using the stereotyped outfits and name. This too has become a discussion among many Native Americans. Some believe it to be "selling out" or "inauthentic" while others argue that it is a taking back of Native power. Regardless of where people fall on this question, the reality remains that the images produced by popular culture shape people's perceptions of certain groups and places.[4]

In the same vein, in *Indians in Unexpected Places,* Philip Deloria writes about Native performers who performed alongside the ethnic impersonators. He argues that some "Native people engaged in the same forces of modernization that were making non-Indians reevaluate their own expectations of themselves and their society." The white performers pulled from the popular genre of "Indian plays," though as Deloria argues, Native performers "surely set and reinforced white expectations concerning Indian gesture, custom, and appearance, but, by and large, their material seems to have emerged from Native cultural practice rather than the fictions of the Indian play."[5] Unfortunately, this added to the confusion that continues to this day about who is Native, as white audiences could not differentiate between the authentic and the impersonation. Since both types of performers presented themselves as authentic, audiences unfamiliar with Native American culture accepted both as an amalgam of true Native performance.

The growth of this phenomenon of Native performers corresponded with the growth of vaudeville in the early 1900s as Americans flooded the theaters to see new professional and exotic acts every week. The increasing popularity brought forth a new spectacle of "Indian vaudeville," which presented Native and non-Native acts on the stage. Indigenous and "Indigenous-identifying" performers "appeared at all points on the hierarchy from big- to small-time houses and on global routes from North America to Oceania, some fleetingly and others for long stretches of their careers."[6] Cora Youngblood Corson, like other Oklahoma performers, became the image of the state in the national eye. The popularity of Native performances drove Cora to present herself as a Native on stage and drove her ever-changing performance to retain her popularity. As she said, "It has always been my belief that to stick to one way of doing things shows that one is not energetic or has no ambition."[7]

ONE

HUMBLE BEGINNINGS

Following the American Civil War, many veterans searched for new ground on which to lay foundations and heal from the war. Many new towns popped up across the West, such as Republic, Missouri. Situated along the St. Louis–San Francisco Railway ("the Frisco") in a thickly populated prairie with excellent local trade, the town quickly boomed.[1] Two of the early settlers, Isaac Tillman Blades and Theodorick Brigit Youngblood, had served in the Union army and settled in the area after the war. Both men had fought in several battles in Arkansas and Missouri, including Wilson's Creek and the Battle of Pea Ridge. They sought new land to start families of their own.

Theodorick Youngblood had fourteen children between two wives, and many of them became involved in business around the town. Theodorick had musical talents, with a fine voice, and in addition to his many positions within the community, he gave singing lessons.[2] One of his sons, Jeremiah M. Youngblood, ran the general store in Republic. He quickly became the "leading merchant" of Republic, though he does not appear to have been well liked by the community.[3] Isaac Blades had a daughter named Sarah Jane Blades. On May 5, 1878, according to Missouri marriage records, Jeremiah and Sarah married.

Jeremiah and Sarah had five children: Ella, Isaac, Anna, Cora, and Eula. Cora Youngblood was born on January 19, 1886. Musical talent continued in the family, and Cora took music lessons from the age of five.[4] These lessons, undoubtedly also taken by her sister Eula, would shape Cora's professional life. The family grew in Missouri, and at the age of fifteen Cora attended school in St. Louis to become a milliner.[5] However, Cora's father began to see advertisements for land opening in the Oklahoma Territory. He saw an opportunity for a mercantile businessman to become rich by taking advantage of the needs of a growing settlement.

Along the south bank of the Washita River in southwestern Oklahoma sat the small Wichita Agency, which administered the affairs of the Apache, Caddo, Comanche, Kiowa, and Wichita tribes in the region. By August 6, 1901, the Kiowa, Comanche, and Apache lands had been allotted and the surplus land would be auctioned to white settlers that day. Homesteads were dispensed on a lottery system, while town lots were auctioned. On the opening day, almost twenty thousand settlers gathered for the auction.[6] The community of Anadarko, Oklahoma Territory, sprang up from the fields surrounding the agency as settlers began to sow their own roots in the region.

Jeremiah Youngblood purchased block 28, lot 15, for $125.[7] He quickly opened a new mercantile business in the growing town, simply named J. M. Youngblood. He sold "dry goods, clothing, shoes, and groceries" and published his first newspaper advertisement on September 26, 1901.[8] As the town and his business grew, Youngblood began to expand his stock with whatever he could get for a good price. By January 1902, he began selling and renting-to-own sewing machines and offering free photo enlargements with any purchase.[9] Clothing, shoes, and sewing machines supplied his family with business and enough income to build a home. With the city growing and the amount of travel to and from the area increasing, luggage became a hot-selling item, which Youngblood gleefully provided.[10] Youngblood himself frequently traveled to add to his stock, including trips to St. Louis to purchase a full line of fall and winter merchandise.[11] The success of the store led Youngblood to begin selling musical instruments, including organs and pianos, which sold for payments of one dollar per week.[12] This decision led to a growth of musical aspirations in the family and Anadarko. Over the next few years, Youngblood expanded the selection to include guitars, mandolins, violins, and more.[13]

As her father, Jeremiah Youngblood, began to expand access to music in

Anadarko, Cora settled into her new life in Oklahoma. The region suffered, like many early western settlements, from a sense of lawlessness. One early settler recalled that in the early years after 1901, "Anadarko was in the grip of the lawless . . . and on one occasion of the convening of court twenty-five cases were on the docket for murder alone."[14] In this rough environment, Cora interacted with the many members of the local tribes, with varying degrees of familiarity. These interactions gave her an observational understanding of Native culture that she would later use on the vaudeville stage.

However, first Anadarko needed to sell itself as a bastion of progress on the Plains, to attract more settlers. On its one-year anniversary, the town declared itself the "Queen City of the Washita," which had grown "from nothing to a beautiful, healthy, law-abiding city of four thousand people, the peer of any community in Oklahoma."[15] A part of the refined growth required cultural institutions such as entertainment venues. For many towns in this era, entertainment came from the opera house, saloons, and local town bands.

In August 1902, sixteen-year-old Cora led "eighteen of Anadarko's brightest young ladies," including her sister Eula as well as Iona Cooley, Florence McAninch, and Ethel Hoaghland, in organizing a brass band. But as Jill Sullivan points out in her book *Women's Bands in America*, "For much of the nineteenth and twentieth centuries, playing in a band was a masculine pursuit." Creating her own band may have provided an outlet for these young women to exercise their independence, freedom of choice, and artistic expression with others, and to be aggressively noisy, perform in public, socialize, and learn to work together in ways that aided their development.[16] The women, situated in a remote town in Oklahoma Territory, sought a creative outlet that let them overcome social ideas about how they should behave.

Rural towns had little opportunity to attend concerts or travel for a performance. A brass band became a status symbol for small communities as it represented economic flourishing. It enhanced the town's quality of life and brought much-needed recognition to the region as the settlers attempted to establish themselves and grow. The bands not only provided entertainment but also played in parades, ceremonies, and even funerals. A band represented the best of the community, and Cora's band certainly illustrated this.[17]

The *Anadarko Daily Democrat* reported that the women were "ready music readers" and sought subscriptions to pay for instruments. The citizens of Anadarko gave liberally, some subscribing ten dollars. On the first day of their

Anadarko Ladies Band. 1902. Cora Youngblood is fourth from the left. Courtesy of the Anadarko Heritage Museum.

venture, the band secured more than $150 of their $600 goal.[18] The girls hoped that by selling these subscriptions as shares of stock in their band, they could easily buy all the necessary equipment. They planned to call themselves the Anadarko Ladies Cornet Band and were being trained by Professor John A. Sager, director of music at Mt. Carmel Institute at Minco, Oklahoma.[19] Members of the band were Cora Youngblood, Daisy Kane, and Eunice Cleveland, who played the cornet; Florence Baird, Mrs. G. W. Keeler, and Miss Eula Youngblood on clarinet; Iona Cooley, Eunice Cleveland, and Lou Daniels as solo alto; Miss Lober, Eleanor Graycia Acton, and Ida Mundell on trombone; Miss Nellie Kennedy on bass drum; and Nora Johnson on snare drum.[20]

Band members also held ice cream socials to raise money for instruments. By September 29, they had raised enough money to procure instruments and had undergone enough practice to begin performing shows for their town.[21] A performance by the Ladies Band garnered a lot of attention and delighted denizens of Anadarko with multiperformance programs that incorporated string, piano, and vocal solos interspersed with numbers from the whole band.

Cora held the final solo position before the band closed out the program.[22] The citizens of Anadarko saw their endeavor as a something to encourage and support because "a place is a 'dead number' indeed without any kind of a musical organization."[23]

Following Cora's example, in October, her father formed a male band of seventeen pieces. In many of the stories involving Cora during her lifetime, we see that despite her accomplishments, men would attempt to eclipse her abilities, or she would be pushed from the actual story. Today, for instance, the Anadarko Philomathic Museum displays a photo of Jeremiah Youngblood and his band, with the caption "The First Band Organized in Anadarko, 1902, by J. M. Youngblood." In addition, the news article announcing J. M. Youngblood's band gives his band much greater praise than was bestowed in the article about the Ladies Band:

> It is a fact that cannot be disputed that there is more stir and progressiveness manifest in a town that has a band than one that has no musical organization. Then Anadarko should be full of it. The men of the town, not to be outdone by the ladies (God bless 'em—the ladies) . . . The members are practicing two or three nights weekly and will soon be able to discourse just as good music as you can hear in any old town. The have purchased nearly all the instruments needed and a little later on will purchase handsome uniforms . . . When they get to making music we'll put 'em up against anything in the two territories.[24]

The band included sixteen men from the community. Of these men, one in particular, Charles Corson, caught the attention of Cora Youngblood.

Charles belonged to the Piegan Nation of Montana. His father, Corporal Schuler M. Corson, Company D, Seventh Infantry, had served in the United States Army in Montana from 1871 to 1877. After his discharge, he remained in Montana and among his other enterprises was the editor of the *Montanian,* published in Choteau, Montana. In 1880, Charles Corson was born from a relationship between Schuler and a Piegan woman. However, Schuler did not include Charles in his family and would only later reluctantly accept Charles into his life when the boy was a teenager. At the age of fourteen, Charles was sent to the Carlisle Indian School in Carlisle, Pennsylvania, where he remained for eight years.[25]

While attending school, Corson played second cornet in the school's or-

Charles Corson.
Author's collection.

chestra, sparking a love for music.[26] He was formally trained as a tailor before graduating in 1900.[27] But music was his passion, and he remained at the school to help with the band and to take a business course. In 1902, he left Carlisle for a job in Anadarko, Oklahoma Territory, as assistant leasing clerk at the Kiowa Agency.[28] He moved into a little cottage near his office and constantly kept busy as the agency served the Apache, Comanche, Kiowa, Wichita, and several small Native bands.[29] Charles saw J. M. Youngblood's band as a perfect opportunity to continue his passion amid his busy work schedule, and it seems that his experience teaching music at Carlisle helped the Youngblood band. In November 1902, Corson wrote a letter to the Carlisle Indian School stating that he "is teaching a band in town during his off hours in the evening. The band is made up of whites and is improving and they are already able to earn something as a band. He expresses great gratitude to 'dear old Carlisle' for the opportunity he had here to learn music."[30] Thus, he grew to know the Youngbloods well through music.

The men's and women's bands occasionally worked together to perform grand shows for the people of Anadarko and to fundraise. At the end of October 1902, Cora played a defining role in one of these shows, which would set the stage for her future career. On the twenty-seventh, a full house greeted the combined efforts of the bands in a production of a five-act comedy, *Tony the Convict,* performed at McAninch Hall, with the proceeds going to the Ladies Band. The price of admission was "25 and 35 cents; children 15 cents."[31] Wonderful reviews followed the evening's performance as "Miss Cora Youngblood, as Mrs. Van Cruger, performed her part splendidly and elicited much favorable comment from the large audience." As a whole, "the performance was better than the average show that make small towns" and special request was made to have it performed again.[32] The businessmen and other who missed the Saturday showing came the next evening with another large crowd. Once more Cora took the spotlight in the newspaper: "Special mention is due Miss Cora Youngblood, who delighted the audience with a vocal selection entitled 'I'll Be There, Mary Dear.' Miss Youngblood is indeed a sweet singer and was vociferously encored at the conclusion of the song." The Men's Band furnished the music for the event and the two groups contemplated taking the show to neighboring towns.[33]

With the success of their performance, a bidding war started among the citizens of Anadarko to have the Ladies Band play in front of their business. Colonel Karl Preger began the bidding at five dollars.[34] Rosy Fant, the proprietor of the Court Bar Saloon, offered ten, which the mayor, William H. Divers, the next day raised to twelve dollars to have the band play in front of the Divers & Taylor firm. Divers stated that he would "not stand for any secondhand man or saloon man outbidding him."[35] The businessmen of C Street combined their money to bid twenty-five dollars to have the band play in the center of their block.[36] To counter, the businessmen of B Street banded together to raise a bid of fifty dollars.[37] This spirited rivalry ended when Preger, the man who started the bidding, won for an unannounced amount. The Ladies Band played in front of his place of business, acquitting themselves creditably. They established themselves as a feature attraction of the city, one that the *Daily Democrat* hoped would be permanent.[38]

For the rest of the year, the Ladies Band performed at various events around the city. On November 3, in neat uniforms, the band marched in a parade through the principal streets of Anadarko.[39] They received invitations to play in neighboring cities such as Bridgeport.[40] In December, they serenaded Reverend Lillie and family. Their popularity in the town continued to grow as the newspapers sang their praises: "The Ladies Band is very popular, not only for the delightful music rendered, but also on account of the charming young ladies of which it is composed."[41] To close out the year, the Ladies Band performed a holiday concert. They played four classical pieces and were assisted by some noted musicians from the nearby town of Minco. The performance was advertised to "eclipse any musical that has ever been given in Anadarko."[42]

The next year, the Ladies Band continued performing in Anadarko at fundraisers and events such as the Anadarko School Board meeting and the Woodman Banquet.[43] The programs would include various recitations, vocal solos, mandolin trios, piano solos, and of course the entire band together. Besides selling tickets to the show, the women would sometimes sell baked goods at an auction. On January 8, 1903, they sold a cake to the highest bidder and their total for the night amounted to thirty-five dollars. The money went toward continuing to employ Professor Sager as their music teacher.[44]

However, both the women's and the men's bands drew criticism from the *Daily Democrat* for charging the citizens of Anadarko too much for admission. The paper cautioned the bands to "be reasonable in their charges to our citizens when playing for them and not charge them every dollar that they will pay." Given the town's generous donations to the bands, especially to the Ladies Band, the people would "get tired of being charged exorbitant prices on all occasions." The paper warned that "the bands must at all times remember that they need the good will and cooperation of the citizens of Anadarko.[45]

On January 14, 1903, the noted orator and twice the Democratic nominee for president of the United States, William Jennings Bryan, visited Anadarko during a lecture tour in the Oklahoma Territory under the auspices of the Knights of Pythias Lodge. Upon his arrival, both bands played to celebrate. Bryan toured the town and gave an impromptu speech to the crowd assembled. At the Windsor Hotel, all the members of the Ladies Band met him.

He congratulated them on "the excellent music furnished" and exclaimed that they "were a credit to any band and he could hardly believe that this band had only been organized a few months." Bryan then gave his speech, "A Conquering Nation," which lasted almost two hours. After his speech, he left the town to continue his tour with the pleasant recollections of "the Ladies' and Men's Band for their excellent music."[46]

A visitor to Anadarko, who wrote a letter to the newspaper signed only "College Student," praised the "soon-to-be thriving western city" for its beautiful location, progressive and successful businessmen, and "some of the fairest of the fair, if the members of the Ladies Band are to constitute the standard from which one is to judge." The anonymous writer then lamented the presence of "two vultures" in the form of a saloon and gambling house and a "variety theater." The "man-made dens of vice" depreciated the natural beauty of Anadarko. Fortunately, the women had created an "organization of which the city may well be proud." Their skill influenced this writer so thoroughly that they ended their letter with "Here is a health to Anadarko and the Ladies Band."[47]

The Ladies Band continued its success with a trip to perform in various nearby towns, visiting Minco and Chickasha as it continued toward Oklahoma City.[48] With their freshened skills, the young women played at various locations, including the headquarters of the *Oklahoman,* which stated that "the fairest belles of the 'new country'" played "the finest music ever heard in the prosaic realm of a newspaper office." However, the article published about the visit of the band incorrectly listed it as the Lawton Ladies Band. This led to a snide compliment by the *Daily Democrat* of Anadarko, which stated "it is a strange coincidence that the names of the members of Lawton Ladies Band are identically the same as those of the Anadarko Ladies Band. We congratulate Lawton upon the possession of such an array of musical talent."[49]

As the year continued, the ladies continued to play and hone their talents. Their success began to inspire other towns. After the band visited the town of Lawton, for instance, the locals underwent a "considerable revival of interest" in forming their own ladies band.[50] Cora also began to spend more time with Charles Corson and they soon became the subject of talk in the newspapers. On April 26, 1903, the two were reported together as sightseers in Chattanooga, Oklahoma.[51] However, after this mention, the record is blank on Cora, Charles, or the Anadarko Ladies Band until March 26, 1904. During this lull,

Cora and Eula Youngblood traveled back to Republic, Missouri, to perform vocal solos at the commencement of Republic High School.[52]

From May to December 1904, the Louisiana Purchase Exposition, informally known as the St. Louis World's Fair, was held in St. Louis, Missouri, to commemorate the 1803 purchase of the Louisiana Territory from France. More than sixty different countries and forty-three of the forty-five states in the union were represented at the fair through exhibitions that drew almost 20 million visitors. The twin Oklahoma and Indian Territories also constructed buildings to showcase their region's accomplishments. The exposition "glorified America's increasing control over the world's natural resources and in particular how business acumen and ingenuity, coupled with scientific and technological know-how, were pushing the United States to the forefront of the industrialized nations."[53] For the average visitor, the draw of the fair was the hundreds of exhibitions.

The fair covered around 1,200 acres with more than 1,500 buildings connected by almost seventy-five miles of roads and walkways. For the average attendee, this sprawling exhibition promoted entertainment, souvenirs, and popular culture, but as historians such as James Gilbert have emphasized, at the center of the fair rested "matters of race and imperialism."[54] The exposition celebrated the seeming inevitability of the white American race's "march of progress."

But even in an exhibition dedicated to a narrative of white progress, Native America pushed back. This is best exemplified by the involuntary appearance of another Oklahoma resident, the Apache chief Goyahkla, popularly known as Geronimo. William J. McGee, anthropologist and chair of the Louisiana Purchase Exposition's Department of Anthropology, claimed that the exhibition would be a failure without the presence of the Apache. Their popularity and presence in the American imagination after their conflict with the United States made them the perfect example of American greatness and superiority over Indigenous peoples. For this reason, McGee secured Apache prisoners from the White Mountain Reservation and Fort Sill, Oklahoma Territory, one of whom was Goyahkla.

Goyahkla's multiple wars in Mexico and the United States and his evasion of authorities had made him arguably the most famous Native American in the country. After his 1886 surrender he became a prisoner of war and was shipped to Florida. In 1888, he and his band of Chiricahuas were moved to Mt. Vernon Barracks in Alabama until 1894, when they were finally moved to Fort Sill to live as prisoners of war. As a prisoner, Goyahkla was paraded around to events, including fairs and parades, by the United States Army.[55]

The 1904 exposition attempted to capitalize on Goyahkla's infamy by heavily promoting his presence, with plenty of exaggeration and hyperbole. Visitors expected to see a man "whose presence made every white settler tremble with fear," with bloodthirstiness in his eyes. However, some reporters presented published articles of a "model" Native, stating that "long years of captivity have broken his spirit, and he is docile because he has met his masters." The public did not know what to expect from seeing this infamous Native, but his attitude proved defiant in the face of prejudice.[56]

After his many public appearances, Goyahkla had learned how to manipulate a crowd and capitalize on his fame. While walking the fairgrounds, he would "cut off and sell his coat buttons" as souvenirs, then sew on another set before repeating the process. He also made and sold bows, arrows, and canes as well as selling photographs of himself. Goyahkla charged for his signature as well, making a handsome profit from his trip to the fair. Many visitors requested "war whoops or other stereotyped behaviors" they expected from him, but he refused. He also refused to wear stereotypical clothing, preferring to dress in Western-style clothes. When confronting upset visitors, Goyahkla would say "God bless you" and then part company.

His actions caused many to complain that this feeble old Indian could not be the Goyahkla of their imagination. Uncertainty arose around Goyahkla and whether Native Americans "could assimilate to Euro-American culture and still remain Indian." Geronimo's refusal to participate in fairgoers' ridiculous requests came from a decision "to not talk needlessly, especially to visitors who were rude or made jokes at his expense. It was not his problem that people wanted a romanticized dime-novel warrior."[57]

Like Native America, Goyahkla could not be forced to assimilate or be removed. Instead, he defiantly stood against the white imagination, even at the heart of their celebration of racial greatness. His appearance at the fair in this manner, as Philip Deloria argues in *Indians in Unexpected Places,* put "two different symbolic systems in dialogue with one another."[58] To the American public, Native Americans symbolized the America of old, but Native people are not stagnant, and even if defiantly, they too progressed with American society. To see a figure like Goyahkla in a modern light fiercely competed with the nostalgic idea of Natives that people hoped to see.

Despite Goyahkla's counter to the theme of the fair, many exhibitions sought to demonstrate "the superiority of middle-class American democracy, capitalism, and culture," with popular culture becoming a necessity for any exhibit to attract crowds.[59] In this, Oklahoma looked to create a huge splash at the exposition. Oklahoma Territory became so invested that it created the Oklahoma World's Fair Association, "incorporated under the laws of the Territory of Oklahoma . . . to give to the people a cheap and easy way to see the great World's Fair at St. Louis."[60] The people of Oklahoma wanted to showcase their territory and make sure that its citizens would be a part of the celebrations. The official perspective of the state was published in the *Pythian Times:*

> Oklahoma will occupy her usual place in the front line at the St. Louis World's Fair, showing to the millions of people from all parts of the world, who assemble there, that this is the most progressive and prosperous community on the face of the earth.
>
> It is the hope and ambition of the Oklahoma Commission that our Territory and our people will stand in their true light before the world—a commonwealth whose resources are great, whose possibilities are unlimited, a people who do and accomplish all things and whose energy, enterprise, and progressiveness are nowhere surpassed.[61]

Promotion of Oklahoma's success reflected the fair's promotion of American successes on the national and international stage.

A large draw for this promotion was the presence of music. Visitors to the fair could listen to thousands of concerts "from the great John Phillips [*sic*] Sousa Band to operettas and the elegant ragtime music of composer Scott Joplin."[62] One of the exhibitions, the World's Press Congress, drew large state delegations from around the country, who competed to draw attention to their respective state or territory. Oklahoma and Kansas were the only delegations to bring bands.[63]

The Oklahoma Press Association sought to have a women's band represent and play for them at the exposition. They selected the Stillwater and Lawton

Ladies Bands along with members of a disbanded group from Edmond to form the Oklahoma Press Association Band under the direction of Professor J. M. Jaynes.[64] Unfortunately, a "sickness and other causes" prohibited the addition of the women from Lawton. This opening allowed Cora Youngblood, Ida Mundell, and Florence Baird, all from Anadarko, to join the Oklahoma Press Association Band.[65]

Cora now had the opportunity to represent the territory's exceptionality through music. The *St. Louis Globe-Democrat* described their attendance this way:

> There is one interesting result of teaching young ladies how to play on brass band instruments. It puts dimples in their cheeks. Oklahoma has brought a brass band to the Fair, composed entirely of young women. The only man in the band is one whom it seems necessary to employ to beat the bass drum. This is where mere man still finds himself useful; and yet it is not likely that he is needed so much to beat the bass drum as it is that someone pretty stout is required to hold up that heaviest instrument of the band. It would seem that the man might be employed only to hold the drum while some fair performer thumped it in proper time. If there is going to be a ladies' cornet band, let there be not one false note in it—not even one man . . . Oklahoma is a wonderful territory and deserves statehood, and if she doesn't get it soon there may be more feminine brass.[66]

This twenty-three-member band performed at the Oklahoma building to a crowd of almost four hundred Oklahoma men and women.[67] On May 17, 1904, on the veranda of the Hall of Congresses, the band played for thousands of visitors. The band remained at the fair for several days, giving concerts with the Oklahoma Troop A Cavalry Band of Guthrie, Oklahoma.[68] The Oklahoma Press Association Band had succeeded in their national appearance.

Interestingly, however, Cora was not alone at the fair. Charles Corson also performed at the fair as a member of Dennison Wheelock's Haskell Indian Band. Wheelock, an Oneida Indian from Wisconsin, had been Richard Henry Pratt's favored student at Carlisle Indian School. Wheelock excelled in music and became an accomplished American Indian composer, conductor, and cornet soloist. He "spent twenty years of his life at Carlisle, Flandreau, and Haskell Institute as a student, clerk, disciplinarian, bandmaster, and professor of music."[69] Wheelock had taught music to Charles Corson during his time at Carlisle, before leaving to teach at Haskell Indian School. This likely resulted in Charles joining the group for the world's fair.

The Haskell Indian Band, the only Indian band hired by the Exposition Company, drew large crowds to their concerts, which were performed twice daily from June 14 to June 25, 1904. They were compared to John Philip Sousa for their skill. Dennison Wheelock's *Aboriginal Suite* introduced the Native dances and war whoops into his music, making it "interesting as a study of genuine Indian music." The skill of the musicians garnered the admiration of the fair organizers, who stated that their work was "most creditable and gives them a right to the place as the one artistic band of the red race." After their engagement at the fair, they began a tour of the country. They planned to play in Chicago, Cleveland, Indianapolis, Philadelphia, and other cities and then return later in the season for another world's fair engagement performance.[70]

Before their June engagements ended, Charles and Cora were married, on June 22, 1904, in St. Louis. The couple declined to say whether their marriage was the climax of a world's fair romance.[71] Symbolically, the marriage of settler and Native would be repeated in three years, during the celebration of Oklahoma's statehood. At that time, interracial marriage with Native Americans, especially if the marriage involved a white woman, was viewed as an affront to many cultural norms. However, Oklahoma's mixed populations, especially in the communities in Indian Territory, took a more socially liberal view on Native and white marriage. Cora simply added Charles's last name to her own, becoming Cora Youngblood Corson, the name that would stay with her throughout her career. Undoubtedly, this close personal connection with a Native husband allowed Cora to learn more intimate details of Native culture through his stories of growing up on the Blackfeet Reservation. His role in the Wheelock band would also have shaped her understanding of performance in Native regalia and how to intrigue the audience with Native settings.

After the fair, there is no record of Cora's whereabouts until August 1905. It appears she may have traveled with the band or settled back in Republic, Missouri, for a time, waiting for Charles's circuit to end. In August, Cora visited her father in Anadarko, but it is not clear from where she came.[72] In a letter from Schuler Corson to Charles dated November 24, 1904, Schuler mentioned that the circuit should end soon. He inquired about Charles' plan, stating, "I suppose you will go to Republic where I suppose Cora is waiting for you, judging from her last letter."[73] Cora and Charles's marriage started with each touring in separate bands, and it would continue this way moving forward. However, Cora's work at establishing her reputation set the stage for her career to blossom.

TWO

THE RISE

The early 1900s was part of the "golden age of bands," with several well-known bands touring the country, the most prominent being led by John Philip Sousa. However, another popular bandleader of the time, Helen May Butler, led an all-women band originating in Providence, Rhode Island. Her accomplishments as a director quickly earned her the title "Miss Sousa."[1] Beginning her leadership career in the early 1890s, Butler slowly expanded her group to follow the popular "military band" style. By 1900, Butler added a manager named John Leslie Spahn, who quickly worked to sell the band as "America's foremost attraction," devoid of men. In fact, his name would appear as J. Leslie Spahn, hiding his gender.[2]

The band quickly garnered fame for its composition of accomplished soloists. Butler's band rose in popularity as they performed at the 1901 Pan-American Exposition in Buffalo, New York, and at the 1904 Louisiana Purchase Exposition. Butler's became known as a musical master who directed one of the best bands in the country. She also married Spahn, on November 5, 1902. On top of this, Butler's composition "Cosmopolitan America" became the Republican Party's official march for Theodore Roosevelt's presidential campaign in 1904. The future of the band and of her relationship looked promising.[3]

However, in 1905 things began to change for Butler. On August 7, Cora Youngblood Corson joined the Helen May Butler band at the age of nineteen.[4] It is unclear how she came to join the band, as several interviews provide contradictory information. One story declared:

> Spahn, manager of the Helen May Butler band, is due the credit for her discovery. Mr. Spahn was traveling through Oklahoma and at Anadarko he heard of this new musical prodigy . . . He was polite with the Anadarko enthusiasts, and more out of courtesy than for anything else he consented to go and see her. Only the fact that she was an Indian maiden, and the daughter of a prominent Indian agent interested him.
>
> The result was that he asked her to play for him. Graciously she granted the request. Her work was a revelation to him. Not only did he find her to be an accomplished mistress of the euphonium, but also a splendid vocalist. He was so delighted with her that he told Miss Butler of her. The band's mistress laughed at him. Her girls twitted him unmercifully about the rustic prodigy who had "taken him in" and made him believe she was a musician.
>
> Then came a time when the regular euphonium soloist of the band was married. This severed her connection with the organization and created a vacancy which Miss Butler found exceedingly hard to fill. The thought struck her that this might be a good time to try Mr. Spahn's find. Correspondence with the girl resulted in her taking a trip east. There she joined the band, and she can remain with it just as long as she cares to stay. She is one of the most valued as well as one of the most popular members of the band. Not only is she popular with the public, but with her colleagues as well.[5]

This story reveals a few things about Cora's early career. She is heralded as a "musical prodigy" as well as an "Indian maiden." This is one of the earliest accounts that describe Cora as being Native American. It also shows part of the cultural bias against performers from the West, with the women in the band insinuating that Cora was a "rustic prodigy" who did not possess true talent. Most importantly, this story reveals Spahn's first tale about Cora's supposed Native heritage, which became the foundation for her career. Spahn and Cora would convince the world that being Native set her apart from the other acts in vaudeville. The idea that Spahn believed Cora was an "Indian maiden and the daughter of a prominent Indian agent" is easily disproven

Cora in the Helen May Butler band uniform. 1905.
Author's collection.

and not something that they could get away with in Anadarko or Oklahoma. However, for the American public outside of Oklahoma, this story made Cora an interesting act worth seeing.

Despite having played the cornet in Anadarko and in the Oklahoma Press Association Band, Cora joined Butler as a baritone player. She quickly took to the new instrument and became quite proficient. After her first concert, Cora received solo parts on an instrument she had hardly played. After only one week, Butler appointed Cora to be assistant director. In explaining her opinion of Cora, Butler stated, "I consider Mrs. Cora Youngblood Corson a phenomenal find. With proper care she will no doubt accomplish great things. I prophesy that she will become one of the greatest, if not the peer, of all lady baritone players. She also has a sweet sympathetic voice that will help her rise above her sister musicians."[6]

Cora's soprano voice also quickly brought her vocal solos in concerts. On October 23, 1905, Cora performed both euphonium and vocal solos during the band's performance at the Olympia theater in Chattanooga, Tennessee.[7] The talents of the women, and especially of Cora, continued to bring high acclaim from reporters and is reflected in accolades from the local news. During a performance at the local Chattanooga armory, for instance, the paper announced that all fans of music should attend to have "the unusual privilege of hearing lady soloists of ability on brass instruments."[8] Due to a continued illness of Helen May Butler, her husband and manager J. Leslie Spahn closed their tour in Cedartown, Georgia, on December 14.[9] This closure provided a life-changing opportunity for Cora Youngblood Corson.

After her stunning performances upon joining the band, Helen May Butler had signed Cora to a five-year contract, from 1906 to 1911, "at a salary far exceeding that received by any other lady musician."[10] However, this may not have been a contract with Butler but with manager Leslie J. Spahn, as later articles point out.[11] Spahn convinced Cora to venture into the world of vaudeville. Up to that point, her only foray into theater had been the play *Tony the Convict,* for which she and her band had performed in Anadarko. This step would take her to an entirely new level of fame.

With her position secured, Cora took her first step into vaudeville with an extension of her role in the Helen May Butler band by performing vocal solos and playing the euphonium. She debuted in Atlanta, Georgia, in January 1906 and quickly found herself discussed in newspapers across the country. An article in the *Atlanta Constitution* stated, "She not only plays her instrumental solos well, but she sings most charmingly." It also declared that the "beautiful and accomplished Cora Youngblood Corson did herself proud at yesterday's performance. She sings like a bird and plays as we have seldom heard The Old Kentucky Home and other popular songs."[12] She quickly garnered fame and the admiration of her hometown.[13]

From the beginning of her career with Butler, Cora had quickly taken to the competitiveness of the profession. In vaudeville, she learned that to continue to top her peers she must constantly adapt. Her novelties changed every few years to keep her act fresh. Her first step into creating a public image saw her donning a decorative buckskin dress while singing popular "Indian songs" of the time. Christine Bold, author of *"Vaudeville Indians" on Global Circuits*, writes that the popularity of Native Americans in vaudeville "attracted large numbers of performers whose claimed Indigenous identities were less clearly grounded." Unfortunately, the context of the times makes it difficult to fully determine whether some of these performers had a true Native heritage or if they simply found it a convenient path to popularity. Bold acknowledges that some cases reveal "an uncomfortable truth that the 'Indian princess' caricature that so endangered Indigenous women in the sexualized binaries it set in motion was sought as a refuge by some non-Indigenous women living closer to the social and economic edge, and sometimes to violence."[14]

For Cora, as Joanna Ross Hersey points out, women musicians in vaudeville faced "an economy where jobs were scarce, and pay was low."[15] Cora likely saw the popularity of Indian songs as a way to use her gender and her connections to Native culture through her life in Oklahoma Territory to her advantage. She dressed in the stereotypical outfit that appeared in popular culture, but she had an advantage that others of her time did not: observational details of Native culture in Oklahoma and a backstory about growing up on an Indian reservation, which could fuel the public's imagination.

The novelty of a Native woman singing and playing the euphonium took her popularity to a new level even within the Helen May Butler band. An advertisement in the *Billboard* magazine dated March 17, 1906, promotes Butler and Cora together. Cora is situated as the "feature soloist" of the band, but she is also endorsed as a "Helen May Butler attraction." The ad markets her as the "most versatile lady musician," whose show is composed of "a refined vaudeville specialty requiring eighteen minutes; opening full stage, closing in one. Introducing quick changes, latest songs, euphonium solos. The only lady known to use this large instrument as a feature. Wardrobe A-1. Booked solid to September 7th, 1906. All time open after that." Finally, the rest of the band was promoted at the bottom of the page. They would start performing on September 8. This reveals Cora's new level of popularity, given her position of equal weight in the advertisement, and indicates that her shows were completely booked for the next seven months.[16]

After performing in Georgia for a couple of months, Cora moved on to Texas for her next vaudeville appearance. The *San Antonio Sunday Light* wrote of her act:

> Miss Corson has the distinction of being the vocal and instrumental soloist of the Helen May Butler band, one of the strongest of the great number of women bands now appearing before the public, particularly in the east. Both of her qualifications to entertain will be displayed at the Majestic. She invests her performance with pleasing costumes indicative of what she is singing. When she appears to sing "Silverheels" it is in the robes of an Indian maiden. Miss Corson closes her act with two solos on the euphonium.[17]

By becoming a Native performer, Cora set herself above other performers by intriguing audiences interested in seeing a "real-life" Native American on stage. After decades of Native American removal to Indian Territory and hundreds of years of interracial mixing, many white Americans could not tell what an "authentic" Native should look, talk, sing, or act like. Therefore, it was not difficult for Cora to convince the American public that she had Native heritage.

The Helen May Butler band soon left Texas and returned to Atlanta, Georgia, to play an April 22, 1906, show to benefit the victims of the San Francisco earthquake. The sheer destruction and size of the earthquake made it one of the most significant earthquakes in recorded history. The devastation called many groups to perform fundraisers to help those in San Francisco rebuild. The band hoped to raise around one thousand dollars for those left homeless.[18] After the performance, the band continued its tour of the principal southern cities.[19]

As the band traveled, Cora's popularity brought her more attention in the newspapers. Widely heralding her as "the most versatile lady musician, vocal and euphonium soloist," papers began to elaborate on her background. The *Birmingham News* wrote that Cora was "a native of Oklahoma Territory, and although but 19 years of age, has been the Feature Vocal and Baritone Soloist in the Helen May Butler band during the past year." Papers like this one presented her as simply a native of Oklahoma Territory, meaning her performance of "Silverleaf," in which she dressed as a Native American, was just an act. She was simply using the Native heritage as a part of her performance.[20]

While the band was in Alabama, Cora began to feature in newspaper advertisements. Instead of Helen May Butler's image, Cora became the star attached to the advertisement.[21] She soon became "a favorite on the vaudeville circuit." In fact, the *Arkansas Democrat*'s advertisement for the Forest Park Theater show included Cora Youngblood Corson as the second headliner, only including the "Helen May Butler Military Brass Band" in small font at the bottom of the ad.[22]

This trend continued into the band's tour. Cora became the prima donna, headlining, while the rest of the band was cast as playing before and after "her" shows. Cora continued to add new acts to her performances beyond the euphonium. She gained "friends at every performance by her sweet singing of ballads and the illustrated songs and moving pictures are fully up to the standard."[23] Cora's willingness to include the latest technology in her performances, such as illustrated songs, which combined music with projected images, illustrates her ability to adapt and remain competitive.

During this adapting of acts, Cora ventured into playwriting and appears to have written her own play entitled *The Red Girl.* While it is not clear what this act constituted, the *Iola Daily Register and Evening News* stated that "Cora Youngblood Corson, the Red girl, will be at Electric Park the week of June 24th." It seems that Cora had begun incorporating a more direct connection with a Native American heritage into her shows through this play. Due to Cora's newfound fame, Electric Park, an amusement park in Iola, Kansas, paid one thousand dollars for the women to perform fourteen concerts.[24] The park was hoping that this unprecedented sum would be rewarded, or at least recovered, as this performance had not been planned beforehand—and it worked. The nightly attendance continued to break records, with the seats "facing the band shell" being filled to capacity.[25]

In July, the Helen May Butler band performed at Wonderland Park in Wichita, Kansas. This new amusement park sought to be the "most popular playground in Kansas and Oklahoma."[26] The park hired the band to perform two concerts a day for two weeks at no cost to the public. The novelty of an all-female band "composed of twenty talented women" became the highlight of the news articles. The news called the band "one of the most unique and at the same time one of the most popular concert organizations in the country," noting that it had previously "played almost exclusively in the east, but this season it has been touring the larger cities of the West with marked success."[27] On their first night, the band played to a crowd of more than two thousand attendees.[28]

On the Fourth of July, the park went all out, decorating in red, white, and blue flags and bunting in profusion. The park reassured the public that its firework display would not disappoint as it had spent more than one thousand dollars to include "bombs, rockets, roman candles, and the most expensive set pieces galore."[29] To match the performances with the fireworks display, extra solos were scheduled to entertain the guests. The overall performance of the band at Wonderland Park garnered praise from the local papers, which remarked that the women were "remarkably good artists in their line."[30]

Once it finished at Wonderland Park, the band performed in Oklahoma City, at Delmar Garden. Created by John Sinopoulo, a Greek immigrant, this amusement park opened in 1902 along the banks of the North Canadian River. Designed in an elaborate art nouveau style, it beautifully blended into the surrounding woods. It offered a zoo filled with exotic animals, an arcade, thrilling rides, restaurants, a floating wedding chapel, a horse racing track, a ballroom, a beer garden, a dance hall, and a three thousand–seat theater.[31] Though neither Cora nor John Sinopoulo knew it, this would not be their only interaction, as their paths would clash intensely in just a few years.

But for the time, the papers praised the "celebrated soloist" Cora Youngblood Corson as a local girl hailing from Anadarko.[32] Interestingly, it did not mention her supposed Native heritage, which for the duration of her career continued to be the case during her performances in Oklahoma. Perhaps she could not pull off the Native woman act in a state where the truth could easily be ascertained by looking at her appearance and heritage. However, this did not reduce her popularity in the state.

After a weeklong engagement, the band moved to St. Joseph, Missouri, for a short time. Reflecting Cora's popularity, the advertisement in the local paper featured a photograph of Cora with the headline "Miss Cora Youngblood Corson, Euphonium Soloist, with Helen May Butler's Ladies' Military Band." They performed at Krug Park for a few days before continuing their tour.[33]

Later in the month, the Helen May Butler band found itself in Dubuque, Iowa, for daily performances at Union Park. The band performed from July 29 to August 5, 1906. While there, Cora's assumed Native heritage found its way into several newspaper reports in Kansas and Iowa, becoming the main attraction of her story. She once again eclipsed Helen May Butler and the other women. In fact, Cora seems to have become the sole point of interest in the band. On July 8, 1906, one of the local Dubuque newspapers, the *Daily Times,* heralded the band's upcoming visit with speculation and stories of an "Indian maiden" accompanying the group. The paper announced the "Helen Mae Butler Band," with the incorrect spelling, stating:

> Of Helen Mae Butler's band, which will be here July 29 to August 5, little need be said. They filled an engagement at Union Park a year ago and made such a hit that the management decided to re-engage them at great expense . . . First among the soloists is Miss Cora Youngblood Corson, an Indian girl, who was discovered in Oklahoma last year by Miss Butler's manager. She is a fine musician and a singer of note, possessing a sweet contralto voice.
>
> A feature of her work is that she appears in her native "Ogalla" singing native songs, which are illustrated with stereopticon views. For the coming engagement at Union Park, management has gone to considerable expense and have engaged Professor Charles Kirner to reproduce the stereopticon views necessary during Miss Corson's performance. A deep interest has been manifested in the Indian girl and indications are that the crowd will be large at all the concerts, two of which will be given daily, one in the afternoon and the other in the evening.[34]

Cora, as a novelty Indian maiden, attracted much of the attention.

The *Dubuque Telegraph-Herald* dedicated several columns over the period of a week to Cora and her heritage, following an Indian maiden trope. She was regarded as "a typical Indian beauty" who was "enjoying her novel experiences with the band to the fullest extent." The newspaper also provided a new backstory for Cora's career with Helen May Butler that emphasized her Native heritage. The tone of the interview suggested a deep affection for Cora on the part of J. Leslie Spahn, the source of the interview, and stated that he "can talk of nothing else but Cora Youngblood Corson, the young Indian girl whom he is featuring with the band."[35]

The article contained many stereotypical tropes when discussing Natives. For instance, Cora is a "young Indian Princess" who had to be won "away from the land of her fathers." It also repeated the idea that she was the daughter of an Indian agent and claimed "she had never made a public appearance." The article also described Cora as a young "Silverheels," referencing the popular Indian song of the time that she performed on stage, and included an image of Cora in her Native garb. The paper stated that "she is dark of skin, and has a perfectly amazing wealth of raven tresses, which form an enchanting setting for her shapely features, of which her sparkling black eyes are by far the most noticeable." Cora likely surprised many visitors who bought tickets expecting to see such a dark individual on stage rather than a tall, white woman. The interviewer also asked Spahn why Cora did not "do her Indian costume act in full during the band concerts," to which he replied, "What would I save, then, for her act in vaudeville?" This is an interesting dichotomy as it states that Cora is herself an Indian but also that it is an act. It appears that the reporters believed Cora was in fact a Native woman performing a musical act.

Cora's horsemanship also came into the discussion. Moving forward, her ability to ride would commonly be mentioned in articles, perhaps adding to her allure as a Native woman who grew up on the rugged plains of Oklahoma. Spahn claimed that "in the little town in Oklahoma where he found her, her equestrian feats were the talk of the town, and if there was a piece of horseflesh anywhere in the country that had a bad reputation, she was up and determined to conquer it."

In the end, the reporter asked how this "young princess who came out of the west" fared when compared to her eastern associates. His response shone kindly on Cora's association with Oklahoma: "While she does not ask anyone to pander to her, or to wait on her, still she has always been so used to pleasant surroundings, that she simply must have a kind word from everyone." This interview securely established Cora's association with the fledgling territory of Oklahoma and her Native image. It spoke to the idea of her representation as a rugged pioneer woman and an elegant Native woman. She became the epitome of Oklahoma's national image in the press.

Though much of the information in the article is incorrect, the attraction of the "young Indian girl" still drew a large crowd. She assumed the role of Silver Heels and presented the citizens of Iowa a remarkable sight: a female Native American from Oklahoma whose performance and appearance would dazzle any crowd.

The desire of white Americans "to consume performances of racial and ethnic differences rendered in musical terms" provided a perfect opportunity for Native musicians.[36] Music became a way to sell the "expectations about Indianness," and Native people "were involved in recording, contesting, affirming, transforming, controlling, and performing those expectations in critical ways."[37] The American public's fascination with Native Americans in the early twentieth century was fueled by the myth of the "vanishing Indian," a self-fulfilling prophecy that echoed the ideology of "manifest destiny." As white settlers expanded westward through territorial conquest and violent displacement, a pervasive cultural narrative emerged, suggesting that Native Americans were destined to fade away through conflict, disease, or forced assimilation. The "growing sentimentalism for the apparently dominated and disappearing wilderness turned Native peoples and places into commodities."[38] This idea sparked the interest in Native performers in the 1900s that Cora used to her advantage when she performed in Native costume.

Whether by design or through connection to her acts, she became even more of a novelty. She was not only an accomplished female musician but also a Native musician. Perhaps the attention to her Native heritage while in Iowa is due to the public's lack of knowledge about Natives. By the eighteenth century, Iowa had seen multiple tribes enter the territory, including the Sauk and the Mesquakie from eastern Wisconsin. The Sauk were later forcefully removed from Iowa into Mississippi, which sparked the Black Hawk War of 1832. Some Potawatomi from Illinois and some Winnebago from Wisconsin were moved into Iowa by the United States Army in 1837 and 1840, respectively. However, by the late 1840s, all tribes were removed from Iowa and relocated into Oklahoma and Kansas.[39] Thus, by the time of Cora's arrival, the presence of a Native American in the state was a novel sight. This likely sparked the intense curiosity and the papers' obsession with discussing her false Native heritage. In turn, the popularity reinforced the reason to perform as a Native, since it continued to keep Cora Youngblood Corson in the news and to draw crowds.

Cora's influence with the public helped the Helen May Butler band become a rousing success for Union Park. On July 29, 1906, the papers predicted that between seven thousand and eight thousand people had visited the park for musical entertainment. The crowds adored the women, giving them more "enthusiastic and vociferous applause" than any other performance that summer. The uniqueness of an all-women band showed, as the *Telegraph-Herald* stated, "It has always been thought that girls could not properly manipulate wind instruments, but the young women appearing at the park this week seem to put this theory entirely to rout." It also continued the praise for Cora's exceptional heritage: "Naturally, there was much interest manifested in Miss Corson, the young Indian girl . . . A curtain has been erected for the pictures which will accompany Miss Corson's Indian song 'Paxinosa' during the remainder of the week." It is also notable that there were four other advertisements for Cora on the same page of the paper as this article.[40]

As the week continued, Cora and the other women continued to bring in praise for their performances. They began to tailor their musical selections to the tastes of the visitors, and the park continued to fill every night. Cora continued to thrill the crowds:

> In connection with the young Indian girl, Cora Youngblood Corson, it might be interesting to remark that she is getting very lonesome for a horseback ride, and if an animal sufficiently spirited can be found, she is going to take a turn at her favorite pastime. The wilder they are the better, and there is very little in the horse line which she cannot handle, at least that is the reputation she has won for herself.[41]

While she was an accomplished rider, the attention drawn to this part of her life likely acted to connect her to a more Native or rugged past. Cora's abilities both on and off the stage added to her mystical story and excited the public imagination of her roots in a rugged territory.

During one performance that week, Cora faced an unfortunate incident while singing her favorite tune, "Back Among the Clover and the Bees." When it was her time to sing, all the lights were turned off except for a single one over her music. During the summer, an abundance of bugs flocked to any faint illumination. When Cora opened her mouth "in the delivery of a round, full note, one of the bugs flew in and she swallowed it." She quickly began to cough incessantly, to the point of choking. After this, Cora performed a different song, "By the Old Mill Stream," because she was "so scared every time she starts to sing, that she is kept almost too busy watching the bugs to remember much about the music."[42] Fortunately, Union Park visitors continued to adore her every performance, even after this embarrassing moment.

Once they finished their engagement at Union Park on August 11, the band moved to White City in Denver, Colorado, to finish up their summer season.[43] After the Helen May Butler band wrapped up its summer tours, Cora returned to the vaudeville stage. Unlike the local Kansas and Iowa newspapers, the *Billboard*, the magazine that reported on her vaudeville work, did not claim Cora was Native American. Instead, as one article claimed, "Miss Corson is a native of Oklahoma." The article also showed three photos of Cora, one in her "band uniform," one in her "street costume," and one in her "make-up for her rendition of Silverheels."[44] The description of her Native American garb as "make-up" contrasts with the Dubuque *Daily Times* claim that "she appears in her native 'Ogalla'" for her performance.[45] This made-up term highlights how newspapers outside of Oklahoma simply reached for whatever Indian connection they could come up with. Since Cora did not have an actual Native heritage, she could not provide actual information to the press.

It is interesting to note that publications written by vaudeville professionals did not consider her to be a Native American. Instead, she was promoted as an act. The professionals saw her as just a performer using the stereotyped acts of the times. J. Leslie Spahn sought to build upon the popularity of this Native American act and quickly secured a new act for Cora, also entitled *The Red Girl,* written by Bob Watt of Philadelphia. The act was "an Indian melodrama condensed to twenty minutes." *The Red Girl* came replete with novel situations and exciting climaxes through three different scenes.[46]

The Red Girl became a success as a feature along the circuit. Cora performed in the act but also continued her vocal and euphonium solos.[47] The *Billboard* took notice, claiming that "vaudeville needs more sketches like The Red Girl, in which J. Leslie Spahn is presenting Cora Youngblood Corson . . . The western papers are lending it their hearty support."[48] Its continued success brought even more women to the act, increasing the number to ten by the end of November 1906.[49] Despite these successes, Cora did not headline during the vaudeville season. She was listed simply as "the noted soprano and euphonium player," while *The Red Girl* got billed as "one of the finest seen on any of the vaudeville stages."[50] Cora needed another change to stay on top.

Over the next few months, Cora began to develop her performance with the addition of something big. To accomplish this, she added the mammoth BB-flat tuba to her repertoire, an instrument considered too large for women at the time.[51] The addition of the tuba, as well as her performance on the euphonium, were even more remarkable when compared to some of the prevailing thoughts of the time. Reviewers typically saw strength, energy, and dignity as masculine virtues and were surprised to see a woman display such characteristics.[52] For instance, a reviewer named W. J. Henderson wrote in the *New York Sun,* "Does anyone wish to see a woman playing the bass drum or an E flat tuba?"[53] Another example comes from a New York conductor who commented in an interview that "women cannot possibly play brass instruments and look pretty, and why should they spoil their look?"[54] Nonetheless, Cora's career seems to overcome these stereotypes and modes of thinking.

By March 1907, her breaking of gender norms seems to have made her work a novelty once again. The *Logansport Journal* urged its readers to see Cora's show at the local Dowling theater. It promised that she "is beyond doubt the most unique and out of the ordinary musical artist on the stage today . . . Although only 20 years old she has accomplished more in the musical world than most of the star male musicians at 30 years of age." Her use of the BB-flat tuba became a fascinating focal point as she not only used it as a solo instrument but its reported weight of forty-eight pounds played into the novelty of a woman tuba soloist.[55]

Following this change in her vaudeville acts came an even larger shift in her career. Instead of returning to the Helen May Butler band after her vaudeville season ended, Cora formed her own female military band. Her split from Butler is a surprise, given Cora's reported five-year contract. However, it seems that her contract tied her to J. Leslie Spahn, as he too left Butler's band to become Cora's manager. According to Butler family oral history, Cora and Spahn likely had a relationship, as he divorced Butler after leaving with Cora.

In May 1907, Cora began contacting her friends from Anadarko to join her new U.S. Ladies Military Band. Graycia Acton, who played the trombone and had been a part of Cora's Anadarko Ladies Cornet Band, left her job at a phone company in Chickasha, Oklahoma, to join Cora in Cincinnati. Once she joined, the band moved to perform at the Jamestown Exposition in Norfolk, Virginia.[56] By June, the U.S. Ladies Military Band had grown to include thirty-five women and found itself at the White City amusement park in Louisville, Kentucky.[57]

The paper advertised the arrival of "Cora Youngblood Corson's band of thirty-five women. It is one of the most celebrated musical organizations in the country."[58] The band quickly become "one of the biggest musical attractions of the season" and performed twice daily, free to the public, for a week.[59] The band's popularity, paired with better weather, encouraged the White City management to engage the women for another week of performances, which included "popular selections, vocal solos and instrumental numbers." Cora's

Cora's U.S. Ladies Military Band. 1907.
Author's collection.

heritage once again became part of the novelty. The paper reported, "Miss Corson is a woman of unique personality, being a full-blooded Indian girl of pronounced beauty, marked talent as a director, unusual power as a singer, and the mistress of a wide range of musical instruments."[60] The success of Cora's band and the other performers brought nearly twenty thousand visitors to the park on June 16, 1907.[61] Once their second week of performances was up, the band moved on to Cincinnati, Ohio.

In August, the U.S. Ladies Military Band traveled to Scranton, Pennsylvania, to perform at Luna Park for a one-week engagement. The band had been secured to play in Scranton "at a tremendous expense and at the cancelation of other bookings," being the "premier ladies' band in the world." Cora's ability to play the tuba was highlighted in the paper columns, which called it "the largest solo instrument in the world." Once again, the band was listed as headed by Cora rather than Helen May Butler, and a woman named Florence B. Mogle was listed as the director for the band during its time in Scranton.[62]

This time, the novelty of a band composed of women became the large attraction in the newspapers. Spahn claimed to have "insisted that all applicants must be of great personal beauty as well as thorough musicians," which would create "the most captivating aggregation of young women traveling the country today."[63] This focus on the women's looks is reflected in the account of the band. They are portrayed as "thorough musicians," but their appearance takes up most of the description: "The girls wear a neat uniform of dark red skirts, white shirtwaists, red capes, and a military cap to match." Cora is described as "a young Indian girl" who "not only possesses a rich soprano voice, but . . . also plays with skill the euphonium, and a double bass tuba, said to be the largest solo instrument in the world."[64] Despite incorrectly stating that Cora was a soprano instead of a contralto, this article highlighted the different avenues that she pushed to interest the public.

The *Scranton Republican* made several remarks on Cora's stature in comparison to men of her skill. The novelty of her performance is captured in descriptions such as "the spectacle of a slim, trim built girl playing a monster double bass tuba was a sight" and in observations that she "plays the big tuba, which few men have conquered."[65] The newspaper did, however, credit Cora with her accomplishments: "Difficult as this instrument is for a deep lunged man to play, Miss Corson succeeded in securing a tone that awakened tremendous enthusiasm in both audiences."[66] With her evolution of acts, the papers transitioned from discussion of her euphonium solos to her tuba playing, calling it "the most remarkable feature of her work."[67]

The band wrapped up its performances in Pennsylvania and headed for Michigan. The U.S. Ladies' Military Band performed at Wolff's Park in Detroit during the week of August 11 to 17.[68] From there, it continued onward to Port Huron, where it played the final week of August.[69] In Michigan, at the end of the season for her concert band, Cora disbanded the U.S. Ladies' Military Band. In its place, she kept six women to form Cora Youngblood Corson and Her Sextette. Though it was short-lived, her first foray into creating a new band that was all her own showed Cora's spirit and drive to succeed against the many odds against her in the field.

From 1905 to 1907, Cora Youngblood's career pushed her onto the national stage. She became a national star as a Native American musical prodigy from the plains of Oklahoma. She outshined and outperformed all others. Her growth and career trajectory were formed through her presentation of a Native American performance, musicianship, and the breaking of gender norms. With her growing fame, Cora became one of the first national stars to represent Oklahoma, and thus her false image as both a rugged western woman and a Native American became what many assumed Oklahomans to be, even before statehood. Cora's growth might even be said to parallel the growth of her hometown of Anadarko, which announced:

> Should the "Queen City of the Washita" continue to grow at this rate, even for one short decade, look out for your laurels, Guthrie and Oklahoma City—you have a rival in the field, a child born on the banks of the Washita, in the land of Caddo, that was a wonder in its conception, a prodigy at its birth, a marvel in its development, and promises to be a modern miracle, in the near future.[70]

While the city boosters promoted Anadarko as a prospering community, Cora's managers promoted her growing reputation as Oklahoma's prodigy, and her professional development dazzled audiences around the country. Cora Youngblood Corson inspired thousands of people with a vision of Oklahoma as a golden land that created powerful and independent people, a state that offered a fair deal. She helped to create a representation of Oklahoman culture on the national stage.

THREE

VAUDEVILLE

During the early years of her fame, from 1905 to 1907, Cora Youngblood became a national star as a Native American musical prodigy from the plains of Oklahoma. Her growth and career trajectory were formed by her performed representation of a Native American, which reflected public opinion about Oklahoma's national image. However, as she evolved her performances, she began to change her persona. At the height of her career, from 1907 to 1916, Cora's Native image was transformed into an Oklahoma-centered persona to draw new crowds and capitalize on popular trends.

During this period, Cora's motives are interesting in that she chose to point out her rugged and wild past in a profession that generally looked for elegance and refinement for women. On top of this, as historian Joanna Ross Hersey points out, "Little is known about women's early experiences in the American musical labor market." Their roles and need to change reflected their struggles "in an economy where jobs were scarce, and pay was low." Most people "associated women on stage with the chorus line and burlesque shows, and this caused women instrumentalists to market themselves in specific ways." Women entertainers constantly emphasized their own high class and professionalism, with attention paid to elaborate costume and presentation. This meant that women like Cora who played an instrument typically associated with men "attempted to come as close to the Victorian ideal as they could while playing a band instrument."[1] Alongside this drive to project an ideal, Cora used her assumed Native persona to find her place on the stage.

Vaudeville, a popular form of entertainment in America, was a melting pot of entertainers of diverse ethnic and racial backgrounds. It offered immigrants and minorities the opportunity to forge a new life on the stage and represented the changing societal norms in American culture. These foreign themes and cultural representation exposed white audiences to ethnic groups they had not encountered or against whom they held typically harsh, racist views. This entertainment sometimes increased positive exposure of minorities such as Native Americans. Audiences began to accept outsiders in new ways instead of harboring bigotry and racism. Vaudeville accomplished this by redefining the American middle class, which had expanded with the industrial revolution. New technology and income allowed the working class opportunities for leisure they had not enjoyed in the past. Family-friendly entertainment meant that families could bring their children into theaters to experience new and exotic performances without the crude forms of burlesque or minstrel shows.

Cora's growing popularity played into the growing consumer culture of the early 1900s. As a woman, she also faced many challenges in finding her own way through a career controlled and operated by men. The idea of racial cross-dressing helped some performers to find a place where they were no longer under the yoke of cultural limitations. By presenting herself as a Native instead of just as a woman, Cora commanded her own image, and it helped her to navigate the business field and control how she would be perceived.

It was during her time in vaudeville that she made the largest impact upon popular culture. In her book *"Vaudeville Indians" on Global Circuits,* Christine Bold argues that despite many authors' failure to discuss the impact of Native Americans in vaudeville, it served as a very important venue for Natives to negotiate "stereotype and agency by ethnic racialized groups."[2] Cora and other vaudeville Indians helped to erase the old stereotypes in public opinion and to create the foundation that other performers, such as Will Rogers, built upon. However, Cora and other ethnic impersonators also created a public misconception of Natives. Audiences saw white performers claiming

Cora Youngblood Corson and Her Sextette.
Author's collection.

Native personae and incorrectly created associations, such as Cora's link of an Oklahoman with a Native.

Philip Deloria argues that the early Native performers "led the way for future generations of Indian performers." They contested expectations and successfully worked to set them differently, creating a unique moment during which these performers reinforced racial stereotypes but also questioned them through musical performance. For instance, Natives such as Tsianina Redfeather and Princess Watawaso "crystalized a sense of surprise among white audiences" with their performances. Incidentally, ethnic performers such as Cora Youngblood Corson also created this phenomenon, since the audiences believed their false representations. If "Indian music was nothing more than savage screeching and howling, mindless poundings of drums and rattles, then what were Indian mezzo-sopranos and baritones doing on the concert stage, singing Native melodies—much less to opera!—to elegant and stylishly modern piano accompaniment?"[3] These Native performers, both real and imagined, played with white expectations. For Cora, it offered an avenue for fame and popularity. Certainly, "playing Indian" was a clever marketing tool. But it is difficult to know just how much of the deception was by design and how much was driven by industry trends. When others made the false connections that Cora was of Native ancestry, she never publicly corrected the myth.

Regardless of the reasoning, Cora Youngblood Corson and Her Sextette premiered at the Bijou theater in Battle Creek, Michigan, on September 23, 1907. Her new act consisted of three attire changes with different scenes. Three of the women played cornets and the other three played trombones, then closed with six pianos. Cora continued to play the euphonium and the BB-flat tuba.[4] The group remained under the management of J. Leslie Spahn and began to travel toward the East.[5] In this new group, Cora's use of Native American themes became a star attraction. The *Wisconsin State Journal* described the act at the Majestic Theatre: "The opening chorus with the seven girls in Indian attire is very pretty, the song, war dance, and buckskin proving a distinct novelty. The horn solos and the instrumental numbers of the sextette win."[6]

By December, the women began their performances in the East at Wheeling, West Virginia, before moving up to Wilmington, Delaware.[7] They began a weeklong performance at the Garrick Theater on January 6, 1908. The newspapers of Wilmington announced that Cora Youngblood Corson and her six Indian maids were due from the Far West.[8] Strangely, they also added a new claim for Cora as the former "leader of the famous Indian Reservation Band."[9] No record can be found of Cora ever being with an Indian band, suggesting this is another press exaggeration or a misunderstanding of her time with the Anadarko Cornet Band. However inaccurate some of their statements, the press did describe the group as "girls from the Golden West," a title it later adopted for its performances.[10]

As Cora's popularity in vaudeville began to grow, her larger-than-life persona fascinated the readers of the *Billboard* magazine. A recurring column, "Observations of the Stroller on Theatrical Life and Environment," told interesting and humorous stories about vaudeville performers. Cora first appeared in the column on July 11, 1908, and filled four of the seven stories. These stories reflected a negative public image of Natives and confirm the idea that Cora used her observational knowledge of Native Americans from her upbringing in Anadarko to create a Native performance. It also showed the difference between the professional vaudeville perception of Cora as an act and that of the public, which saw her only as a Native woman. Highlighting this, one of the stories detailed how she created *The Red Girl* and acquired her buckskin dress:

> Cora Youngblood Corson, who is now playing vaudeville time in The Red Girl, has a fond of reminiscences anent the manner and customs of the Indians of Oklahoma, her native State . . . She knows the characteristics of the race she has studied at close range. They are shiftless, lazy and improvident. It is most fortunate that the Government will not allow them to dispose of their lands.
>
> It was this intimate knowledge of the red men's and the red women's habits and peculiarities that first gave Miss Corson, who is a musician of considerable note and versatility, the idea for her sketch, which she calls The Red Girl. While she was framing up the act and considering the matter of costume, she recalled having seen on her last visit to Oklahoma an Indian squaw with a dress and shawl that she felt would, in themselves, as novelties, be sufficient to make the act a success . . . So, Miss Corson sought out the abandoned squaw and bought the costume she wanted.[11]

These stories showcase the negative perception of Natives and Oklahoma in the public image. The *Billboard*'s readers saw an image of squalor for Native Americans and Oklahoma while the public saw the elegance and exoticism of Cora's heritage on the stage. However, the tone of the article also shows the key point of Cora's actual identity: She does not identify as a Native. Instead, she makes a clear delineation between herself and the Native "squaw." The negative racial discussion also furthered the separation between Cora and the Natives the article discussed.

By July 12, 1908, the women returned to Louisville, Kentucky, to the White City amusement park where Cora had performed with her U.S. Ladies Military Band the year prior.[12] The next month, Cora and her sextet traveled to Indianapolis, Indiana, performing at the Wonderland theater. Here, the *Indianapolis Star* revealed the complicated issue of representation in local papers. Cora is claimed to be "an Indiana girl of beauty and intelligence," which appears to be a confused reporter attempting to report her as an Indian woman, as many papers had done in the past. However, the article does give one of the best descriptions of the group's vaudeville performance:

> Beautiful costumes, gorgeous scenery, and a miscellaneous glory of light and color combine to make the Cora Youngblood Corson Sextet one of the most magnificently staged acts in vaudeville . . . The act is divided into four scenes,

> each beautiful in itself, but arranged so that they lead up to a climax of beauty. The first scene presents an Indian camp, and the girls, dress in Indian costume, sing a characteristic song, and gracefully perform a characteristic dance. The next scene is a soldiers' camp. The girls are arrayed as soldiers and play military music on brass instruments. This scene merges into the third, which presents a battlefield. The music is again instrumental, the girls giving a musical picture of the battle. The fourth scene, one of the most gorgeous ever staged, shows the girls as animated flowers. The scene is opened by Miss Corson with a tuba solo "Asleep in the Deep." In this scene the girls were forced last night to respond repeatedly to encores.[13]

The Cora Youngblood Corson Sextette now became a novelty for the extravagance of its vaudeville performances. The performance drew upon multiple popular trends of the time, such as the themes of Indian maidens and military scenes. The popularity of composer and director John Philip Sousa at this time saw brass bands performing more military-style marches. Likewise, the growth of America's fascination with Natives, spawning from the ideas of the "vanishing race," meant that Cora's act had something for all viewers. Finally, the extravagance of her performances, such as the performance as animated flowers, meant that her show could draw a crowd eager to be entertained with a constantly changing act.

Of course, some issues did arise with the sets, especially with the Indian village set that the sextet used while performing the Indian songs. The *Billboard* related one such story:

> When Miss Corson's sketch was first produced, she experienced considerable difficulty with the stagehands on account of the care and accuracy required in setting it. The tepees had to be placed just so, and sometimes in the very middle of the act one of them would topple over. To obviate this, a fine wire was attached to the center pole of each of the tepees, and they were lowered from the loft, the wires being secured above.
>
> One night, when the act was being set, one of the stagehands was struck by the pole from one of these tepees which fell from the loft and knocked insensible. No one noticed it, and when the curtain went up, and the lights were flashed on, there he lay, unconscious on the ground, with his arms af-

fectionately around the campfire. It was the comedy hit of the evening with the audience."[14]

Another story in the *Billboard* was related to the set, in which Cora reported:

> After laying off out home in Oklahoma City, I called my act together and placed it at the North Avenue Theatre to put in shape. The opening night all was excitement, and the stagehands lost their heads early in the act, and things began to go bad with the 6-drops that are used. Just before the battle scene in Cavalry Charge, the solo cornetist was hit and knocked out by the roll of the curtain coming down on his head. When the stagehands saw what they had done they pulled the curtain back up again, taking with it one of the girls' dresses, leaving her in no shape to appear on the stage. Down went the curtain again, everybody was yelling up, up; and up went the curtain again, taking the plume drop with it. The audience started laughing, for the drop in one had gone up and down four times, neither time reaching the floor or the flys. Manager Paul Sittner came flying back on the stage and demanded to know what was the matter with the act. I told him that he had heard the girls rehearse, and it was no fault of the players, but that the scenery was not handled properly. He looked around for a moment, then yelled out: "Why in the h-ll didn't you rehearse the scenery?"[15]

In October 1908, Cora once again became a topic of discussion in *Billboard* magazine. From the vaudeville perspective, she claimed to be "an Indian girl, hailing from Anadarko, Okla."[16] Thus, in the eyes of the national public and the top vaudeville magazine, Cora was Native American, which made her accomplishments a representative example for Natives across the board. During this early period of her sextet in vaudeville, however, the press in general did not focus on any supposed Native heritage. Instead, while the group was playing the Montauk Theatre in Passaic, New Jersey, the *Passaic Daily Herald* described Cora as "a handsome young woman of extraordinary height and a pure Grecian profile. She appears in the first number dressed as an Indian and sings one of the latest Indian songs." This is the first time a paper had commented on the complexion of her skin. She appeared to them not as a Native

American but rather as a white woman wearing Native costumes. The paper concluded that the magnificence of the act's costumes and talent made it "one of the neatest acts in vaudeville." Upon completion of the engagement, the paper announced the group had "more than fulfilled expectations."[17] After their performance in New Jersey, the sextet traveled to New York City, where it sailed to Havana, Cuba, for a six-week engagement.[18]

After the completion of its first performance outside of the continental United States, the act returned to New York and immediately began touring. Back in New Jersey, Cora Youngblood Corson and Her Sextette, "from Oklahoma City, Oklahoma," performed selections from *Lucia di Lammermoor* and Cora played the "largest instrument in the world, the Double Bass Tuba."[19] Over the next few months, the group performed in New York, New Jersey, Massachusetts, and Connecticut, without any remarkable promotion. It was given equal weight to the other acts in much of the advertisement. However, a couple of exceptions found their way into the papers.

In Fall River, Massachusetts, the local paper announced the arrival of "the Cora Youngblood Corson Sextette, 'The Girls from the Golden West,' six Oklahoma misses, headed by the daughter of Chief Youngblood of the Ogallallas."[20] This is one of the earliest instances in her career with the sextet that calls direct attention to a specific Native heritage, and the first to suggest she is the daughter of a chief. The reference to "Ogallallas" is reminiscent of 1906 *Daily Times* article from Dubuque, Iowa, that said Cora appeared "in her native 'Ogalla.'"[21] However, Chief Youngblood and the Ogallalla tribe did not exist. Perhaps the reference was to the Oglala Sioux, or it may have been that the eastern papers misread the previous articles and expanded upon them. Either way, it is a strange claim that highlights the confusion around Cora's actual identity as well as the success of her public-facing attempts to create a Native persona.

In Hartford, Connecticut, the *Hartford Courant* announced the uniqueness of Cora's act, stating, "One comes out into the limelight and plays on a bass horn so long that there is not much of the girl visible as she plays it."[22] Cora's ability to solo large brass instruments as a woman had taken on a new novelty. Men had attempted to explain how she could be just as good as, if not better than, some male tuba players. In October 1909, *Variety* published an article that claimed, "the scientific division of Harvard College" had investigated and pronounced Cora's lungs to be "abnormal" and informed her that she would need to develop the upper portion of her body to accommodate the abnormally large lungs. They blamed her "condition" on her continual playing of the euphonium and concluded that "constant blowing has brought Cora and the lungs to a point where the physicians say that though weighing only 145 pounds, she has a development in her breathing apparatus equal to that of any man."[23] A 1910 article in the *Kalamazoo Gazette* declared that Cora continued to play daily "in spite of the . . . brilliant medical men."[24]

As a testament to her lung power, the *Billboard* published a humorous story about the downside to this power:

> The chest development of Cora Youngblood Corson is conceded as phenomenal, the scientific decision of physicians being that she has lungs as large and powerful as either Jeffries or Johnson. Theatrical and musical papers have given much space to the subject from time to time, but any one not knowing Miss Corson would never suspect that this tall, slim girl, weighing 145 pounds, was possessed of this extraordinary set of noise producers.
>
> Several weeks ago, Miss Corson was in Oklahoma City. While there she decided to augment her wardrobe by purchasing a new winter suit . . . The proprietor, seeing that his chatter was of little avail, finally hauled out a suit which, while it pleased Miss Corson was somewhat too small for her. As she emerged from the dressing room, the proprietor said:
>
> "My dear madam, never was a dress made to fit such a superb form as you have. Look at that dress (hailing a saleslady). Wouldn't she make a model, though? Oi, yoi, such a model!"
>
> But Miss Corson, not able to stand his flattery, or the dress, which was too tight, any longer said: "I must get this dress off quick, or it will be torn." The proprietor laughed, saying: "My dear lady, it would be impossible for you to tear that dress. It is not as flimsy as yours."
>
> Miss Corson, not at all pleased with this retort, assured him that by taking a deep breath, she could "rend asunder" his elegant gown, and offered to try, with his consent. It was finally agreed that if she could even as much as rip the garment, he would make her a present of $5.00 in addition to the dress. A long breath, the sound of ripping goods and buttons flying here and there, convinced the proprietor that he had lost. After she had left the store, the proprietor said to one of his clerks:
>
> "Model, hell. She would be better as a bellows in an iron foundry."[25]

Cora's story humorously highlighted her power and skill while endearing her to the public.

The power of her lungs and her ability also spawned beneficial sponsorship. By this time in her career, the C. G. Conn company had taken an interest in her prowess and novelty as a woman that promoted brass instruments, especially the euphonium and tuba. Conn would use Cora as a walking advertisement by furnishing the horns for her band and gifting her elaborate instruments. By December 1909, the company had made a "jeweled euphonium set with 25 diamonds, 176 rubies and emeralds" for Cora.[26] Cora soon became the most prominent woman featured in Conn advertisements and remained so for the next twenty years. Cora also had the company create the largest recording bell in the world for her sousaphone, which she incorporated into her routine alongside her BB-flat tuba. The 1910 *Kalamazoo Gazette* article also announced that Conn had decided to place the large-belled instruments into their regular line of products and call them Corsonphones.[27] However, this never came to fruition.

On top of her work with C. G. Conn, Cora and her sextet were featured on the cover of the sheet music for "Cowboy, Nowboy" by Sam Lewis and Leo Bennett. Published in 1909, the theme and cover of a cowboy paired nicely with the "girls from the golden West." The cover featured the words "Sung with great success by Cora Youngblood Corson Sextette," with an image of the women in military costumes.[28] This added to Cora's repertoire of unique music. She had continued to play composer John N. Klohr's "Corsonian Polka." Perhaps the fact that a favorite of Helen May Butler's band was Klohr's "The Billboard March" connected Klohr with Cora.[29] Klohr would continue to write music for Cora's band and later wrote "The Corson Grouch" for her.

In 1910, the sextet continued its tour in the East before heading west to Chicago. The girls from the golden West drew crowds with Cora's jeweled euphonium. The *Billboard* announced, "This act is possessed of the largest and most valuable euphonium in the world . . . They are said to have created a riot in the East."[30] As the month ended, so too did the vaudeville season for Cora and her band. During this break, the women returned to Oklahoma to spend the summer with their families, enjoying picnics and trips to the city without the stress of performing.[31]

Cora's euphonium. 1909.
Author's collection.

In January 1910, Halley's Comet made its appearance in the sky and created mass public interest. The bright comet could be seen by the naked eye in the daylight, and fascination with the phenomenon inspired many to pen novels and music. Following this trend, Cora wrote "a miniature musical comedy" titled *The Tale of the Comet.* In May, she performed the comedy at the New Theater in Baltimore, Maryland, alongside Mabel McKinley, the niece of President William McKinley.[32]

In October, the Cora Youngblood Corson Sextette kicked off its next vaudeville season with headlining performances at the Folly Theater in Oklahoma City. The theater advertised the group as the best vaudeville performance of the upcoming season. The sextet performed two twenty-minute shows nightly.[33] The background of the women became the novel part of their performance: "The fact that all of the girls are native of Oklahoma and spent most of their lives on ranch in western Oklahoma makes the act one of special interest."[34] Their gender and background made them of particular interest in the context of social norms of their day, but they could not rely solely on a Native representation to carry their popularity. While they were in Oklahoma, the papers did not mention anything about a Native American heritage. Perhaps this is more evidence for the idea that Cora could not pull off a Native image in the state due to the public's firsthand knowledge about Natives. After leaving Oklahoma City, the group moved north to Illinois, where Cora's assumed Native heritage came to the forefront. In Joliet, the paper announced the group's performance at the Grand theater by stating that Cora "is a full-blooded Indian." The newspaper also contained a caricature of the women in Native garb.[35]

In February, the group performed in Mansfield, Ohio, at the Orpheum. While there, the papers announced that it was "the big noise on the bill." The paper also described some of the show: "Emerging from their wigwams the six girls dressed as squaws give an Indian dance and war song about the campfire." As for Cora, her "final effort is a rendition of Rocked in the Cradle of the Deep with an instrument that resembles a foghorn and which serves the purpose perhaps of hiding her completely.[36] In Ohio, wherever they went, "everyone [was] talking about the 'Girls from the Golden West.'"[37] Cora's Native representation came complete with stereotypes in dress, culture, and environment.

In November of that year, while in Pennsylvania, Cora decided to drop her Native act. Instead, she changed her program to feature new "exotic" acts. In Pottsville, Pennsylvania, the sextet performed at the Slater Theatre, where, the paper announced, "the Cora Youngblood Corson Sextette remains for the entire week, and they have changed all their music. Instead of the Indian number they now have a Spanish song, and they play new selections on their brass instruments for a finish. Miss Corson and one other young lady play the Scotch bagpipes, another the brass drum, and two other dance a Scotch dance."[38] Interestingly, they had swapped their Native performance for a Spanish and Scottish act. This change confirms that Cora's performance as a Native was just a performance, not tied to any cultural identity. It was just another method to remain popular. This also can be seen in the advertisements for Cora, which featured a multitude of costumes in a single image. Perhaps this change came as a natural evolution as her Native acts became stale to the audience, or even to her performers. In changing her performances, her act could remain interesting to the audience.

In 1911, the band traveled to the Northeast. As the Easter week attraction, the sextet performed at the Colonial Theatre and was billed as the "biggest act ever brought to Annapolis." They brought with them "more scenery than some of the regular shows that play Annapolis."[39] Their run was commended by a local critic, who stated, "The performance of Miss Cora Youngblood Corson cannot be described adequately—one must see and hear her perform to be fully convinced that she is the acme."[40] While in Maryland, Cora's Native heritage garnered one mention by the paper, which stated she "is of Indian blood," even without her Native performance.[41] For the rest of the year, the sextet continued its new act to great success.

The next year, 1912, took the group into Ottawa, Canada, for the Sherbrooke Fair, known as "Canada's Great Eastern Exhibition."[42] It then continued a Canadian tour through the Bowmanville and Lindsay fairs, both in Ottawa, before returning to the United States.[43] This kicked off Cora's approach to a high-profile career, when she became a truly popular celebrity, the first from the state of Oklahoma. She started to grace the covers of popular magazines. On May 18, 1912, she adorned the cover of *The Standard and Vanity Fair*. On August 30, Cora graced the cover of the *Player* magazine, which celebrated her success:

> Cora Youngblood Corson, soloist and proprietress of the Cora Youngblood Corson Sextet, is a native of Anadarko, the Indian reservation of Oklahoma. She is self-taught, and plays solos on euphonium, tuba, cello, piano, and bagpipes. She is credited with being one of the most versatile lady musicians in the world. By the way of variation she writes, having written "The Red Girl," "The Israelite," and "The Tale of the Comet," and for musical papers under the title of "A Girl Musician." The sextet is celebrating its hundredth week this week.[44]

The group had performed for one hundred consecutive weeks, a remarkable feat for any musician. But Cora did it all, in the public imagination, as a Native from an Indian reservation.

That same day, August 30, Cora appeared on the cover of *Variety* alongside sextet members Graycie Acton, Lois Land, Ida Mundell, Ethel Wright, and Eula Youngblood. *Variety* also celebrated the band's one hundredth week and published the same blurb as the *Player.*[45] The next day, Cora was published on the cover of the *Billboard,* which also celebrated her accomplishments.[46]

After returning from Canada, the group continued to travel across the Northeast and Midwest. It then began to move back to Oklahoma for a well-deserved rest during the holidays. While back in Oklahoma, the women performed for their local fans. On December 27, 1912, the group performed at the Anadarko Opera House for one night. The paper expected the performance to be greeted by an overflowing house.[47] Owing to the women's fondness for their home state, the group performed for rates lower than expected for a show of their skill. The papers reported that it was "surprising to see such a high-class act presented at a theater with such moderate rates of admission." Their admission ran about twenty cents when they could easily be charging more than a dollar for tickets. However, the women performed to the best of their abilities and showed their western roots with their cry:

Rickety, Rickety, Rickety Russ
What in thunder is the matter with us?
We are the girls from the Golden West
Wherever we go they like us best,
Razzle, dazzle, hobble, gobble,
Biff! Boom! Bah!
Corson Sextette, Rah! Rah! Rah![48]

The band then traveled to ring in the New Year in Tulsa, Oklahoma. As part of the city's New Year's celebrations, the Hotel Tulsa held a cabaret where Cora Youngblood Corson's sextet received "encore after encore" for their performance.[49] The next night, Cora and her group performed as the "big feature" at the Wonderland Theater with an all-female bill. In response to this, and the talent of the acts, the *Tulsa Daily World* commented that the "suffragette movement gets a big boost in this show." However, it also made sure to compare the women to male counterparts, such as the description of Katherine Selsor as "a female monologist, who is just as funny as any of the celebrated male entertainers of this sort."[50] As the suffrage movement grew, Cora's gender would become a larger talking point with regard to her career, while her performance as a Native and as an Oklahoman would remain a part of the discussion.

Through January, Selsor traveled with Cora and her sextet into Arkansas and Louisiana. In her act, Selsor would perform *The New Woman,* which "burlesques the suffragette idea that is at its height in the feminine mind." Cora continued her tried-and-true method of "solos, duets, trios, quartettes, and sextettes" while continuing the trend of performing songs from operas, such as the sextet from *Lucia di Lammermoor.*[51] As usual, the physical beauty of the sextet continued to occupy a large portion of the articles on their performance, with reporters jealously telling of their beauty as noted by those "lucky enough to gain admission back stage." Or, as one reporter for the *Shreveport Journal* commented, "The six members of the musical team not only were capable, but several of them had good looks, also."[52]

As the group toured, it continued to change its routine by adding new scenes and even new instruments. One advertisement for the show in Spokane, Washington, on May 24, 1913, mentioned "the mermaid scene is said to be beautiful. There are song and dance numbers and solos played on the weird instruments." They also added a scene of "a battle at the Brooklyn Bridge in New York, and showing the bridge being destroyed by battle ships."[53] Cora also added to their repertoire a new composition by John Klohr called "Corson Grouch."[54]

This article also highlighted their gender with the subtitle "Feminine Musicians Promise Novelty."[55] Another change came that month with the departure of Cora's sister Eula from the band. Eula had performed with Cora since the beginning of her band in Anadarko and the formation of her band after leaving Helen May Butler. Eula left the band in Chicago "with plenty of rice and old shoes" to return to Anadarko to marry Glenn Condon. Condon would grow to be a leading politician, journalist, radioman, and editor of the *Vaudeville News.* They married June 15, 1913, in Tulsa, Oklahoma.[56]

Shortly after Eula's departure, Cora and the remaining five women were featured on the cover of the *Player* and given a page dedicated to Cora's career. The article heralded this group that "breezed into Vaudeville from the

"Corson Grouch." 1914.
Author's collection.

Western Plains" and discussed their "interesting history in the field of American amusements." This article showed the novelty of Cora and her group of women, who came from the American West to dominate the vaudeville stage with a production unmatched by even the best acts.

> One does not commonly associate music and the fine arts with the West. Years ago, the westerner would have gloried in this fact—and even today a lot of those hardy people of the plains and majestic mountains who bank most upon action are just as well satisfied that it is the "Effete East" and not

the "Wild West" which is recognized as the home of this particular kind of culture and refinement.

The history of Cora Youngblood Corson and her associates in the musical sextet which bears her name illustrates in a somewhat striking manner this spirit of antagonism which is suggested by the pitting of the East against the West in music as one of the fine arts. A spirit of antagonism indeed, for it follows that, since there are exceptions to all rules, the West is by no means without its champions in the arts—and champions who have been persistent in their demand for recognition.

PLAYED WITH INDIAN GIRLS AND SQUAWS

Cora Youngblood Corson was born in Republic, Mo., but at the age of ten years, in company with her parents, removed to Anadarko, Okla., then a "rag," or tented, city which had sprung up at the time of the rush for virgin prairie land. Her earliest recollections are of the western plains, her playmate for five of the most important "playing" years of her life were Indian girls and squaws, and she is consequently proud to herself a pure and unadulterated product of the free and breezy West. In those early days of Miss Corson's residence in Anadarko, indeed, there was a time when there were but sixteen white women and six white girls in the "city." Incidentally, it may be mentioned that four of these six girls became members of the original Cora Youngblood Corson Sextet and are still associated with it.[57]

While this article features a few incorrect details, the overall opinion of the act places them in the context of vaudeville. The term "squaw" is an offensive ethnic, racial, and sexist slur for older Native women. Its common use in statements like this quote separate Cora from association as a Native American. This interview also points out, for the first time definitively, that Cora was not a Native but rather a white woman who had moved into Anadarko. Even though this article only saw the light of day for those White Rats Actors' Union members who subscribed to the *Player*, it shows that within the vaudeville circles it was understood that Cora was an ethnic impersonator. But to the rest of the country Cora would continue to be seen as a Native American.

After the departure of Eula, "the girls of the golden West" began a tour on the Pantages circuit, which took them into Canada before they returned to the

Pacific Coast of the United States. The novelty of female musicians, extravagant sets, and impressive musicianship continued to grace the newspapers.[58] The advertisements of this period focused on the group's relation to "the West" and how it had shaped the members' ability. The *Vancouver Sun* noted that the women were "all western born and bred, with the easy freedom and independence of the west in their healthy young bodies." The article also mentioned their unmatched skill and rising popularity. "They are under the personal direction of Cora Youngblood Corson, and so well has she trained them that the 'Girls of the Golden West' Sextet are rapidly becoming famous throughout the whole of America."[59] The tour along the Pantages circuit brought the group back to the United States later in June, where they performed in the Northwest, through Washington, Oregon, Montana, and California.

At the end of its tour in California, the band moved East and prepared for the band's expansion. They performed so well on the tour that Alexander Pantages contracted the group for an even larger production.[60] The new contract increased the band to twelve women, called Cora Youngblood Corson's Instrumentalists. In preparation, the group had already been booked from December 1913 to May 1914.[61] More women traveled to join the organization. Hattie Acton, Graycia's sister, traveled to Kansas City to meet and join the band as it traveled from California to New Jersey.[62] During their journey the group stopped in Tulsa, Oklahoma, to perform on August 1, 1913, at the Empress Theatre.[63] It performed in Illinois, Missouri, and Kansas before stopping in Chicago to celebrate Christmas. During this short break, J. Leslie Spahn arranged a Christmas tree at the Demig Hotel with 160 presents from the homes of the women. Many of the presents contained food, which was used to prepare a big feast for the band to celebrate. Owing to the band's popularity across the country, the packages "came from Oklahoma, Rhode Island, Wisconsin, Massachusetts, and Indiana."[64]

In February 1914, the women traveled to New Orleans, Louisiana, where they performed and participated in a Mardi Gras costume competition. Eula Condon had traveled with the band to Louisiana. She won the "most complete costume" competition with a "beautiful Indian costume, made by a Comanche squaw in Oklahoma, and decorated with Elk's teeth."[65] Cora and the women, as a group, won a second place prize of ten dollars from the Joseph Schwarz Company.[66] This perhaps best illustrates the idea that Cora understood the public's desire to see Native Americans as purely an entertainment.

Cora Youngblood Corson's Instrumentalists. 1915.
Author's collection.

In June 1914, the women began a two-month vacation to return home and visit their families. Cora, Ida Mundell, and Grace and Hattie Acton returned home to Anadarko.[67] In August, the women prepared to travel to New York City to begin a contract that would take them back into Canada.[68] On October 3, Cora became a household name once more as she graced the cover of the *Billboard* magazine. The city of Tulsa announced that "Tulsa may again place on the map this week when the entire front page of the Billboard, the world's greatest amusement publication, was taken up with a portrait of Cora Youngblood Corson, the noted lady musician." The article also announced that a "100-piece Indian girl's band would be taken to the world's fair at San Francisco next year by Cora Youngblood Corson and it will be known as the Tulsa Indian Girls' Band. Every member of the organization must be of Indian descent." Reportedly, Cora would begin rehearsals in January 1915, and J. Leslie Spahn had already secured a contract from the exposition authorities. It would have been "the largest exclusive ladies' band ever gotten together in the world."[69] It is unknown what happened to the plans for this band, which never came to fruition. Nevertheless, the potential for such an organization reveals Cora's continued use of Native American imagery to bill her acts as exotic and unique.

The new year started off with a tour through the Midwest. Through Indiana and Minnesota, the band became a hit and continued to perform for packed theaters.[70] In Minneapolis, Cora gave an interview about her life in Oklahoma and her career playing brass instruments:

> I lived in Western Oklahoma . . . Few girls in that country have ever tried to do anything in the music world, but I know a number of them that would have made the public take notice if they had started out as I did. For they have the lungs and strength that is given those that live in the open in God's country.
>
> If only mothers could see their girls as I see them, thin-waisted, small chests, and sickly-looking faces, and for no reason except that they don't get the fresh air and don't exercise their lungs.
>
> A wind instrument costs all the way from $25 to $125, but that is only a small part of what a lot of people pay to doctors every year for their girls. If ever I quit this business, I intend to start a health resort for young girls with weak lungs and I know that all it will take to make them big and strong will be a lot of outdoor work and a big horn.[71]

The tour took the group back into Canada, and it appears that it expanded the Oklahoma theme. Beginning in Alberta, Canada, the Cora Youngblood Corson Instrumentalists played alongside "Oklahoma Bob" Albright.[72] As a professional singer, Albright had changed his name to Oklahoma Bob instead of "the male Melba."[73] He had formerly been a member of the Lew Dockstader's Minstrels before expanding his solo career.[74] His change in name was likely spawned by a rise in interest in Oklahoma-themed acts such as that of Cora and of Will Rogers. The act returned to the United States on the Pantages circuit through Washington state, where it returned to theaters it had played the year prior. The papers heralded the group as "the best musical act now circling the Pan route."[75]

Once more, Cora's ability became the talk of the papers, alongside her desire to establish a health resort in Oklahoma:

> Why shouldn't the "champion lungs of the world" be owned by a woman who devoted most of her spare time to coaxing haunting melodies out of huge, kinky, and rotund brass instruments?

> Miss Corson attributes this fact chiefly, of course, to her addiction to wind instruments, but primarily to the fact that she was born and raised on the wind-swept plains of Oklahoma, where the ozone is to be had just as nature distilled it. She is decidedly athletic, tall, and handsome. She can ride a bucking broncho until the girth about the equator of the cayuse breaks from its plunges. It is declared, and not denied, that she has a greater chest expansion than any of the present-day champions. Her lung development has been declared by men versed in anatomical mysteries, to be a wonder of the medical world.
>
> She is a living, breathing, walking, and talking advertisement of the fact that the open plains of the great west are God's country, she says, the land of health, happiness, and prosperity. She declares Oklahoma and a wind instrument will make lungs for those who have none.[76]

Ever the performer, Cora's comments brought attention not only to Oklahoma and the West but also to her seemingly inhuman ability. During a performance in Seattle, Cora told the crowd that she planned to open a school to help people afflicted with tuberculosis. She would "retire from the stage before long and when I do the school will become a reality. I aim to found the institution on my 160-acre ranch, near Anadarko, Okla."[77]

In June 1915, Cora received one of the highest honors of her career. The band took its tour down the Pacific Coast into California to attend the Panama–Pacific International Exposition in San Francisco, also known as the 1915 World's Fair. On June 3, 1915, the State of Oklahoma celebrated "Cora Youngblood Corson Day" at the fair to "honor the noted Oklahoma girl." In celebrating, Cora and her group held an all-day open house at the Arkansas and Oklahoma building at the fair, where Cora performed solos on the "euphonium, cornet, trombone, bagpipes, cello, and other instruments."[78] To commemorate the event, buttons and hand mirrors were adorned with Cora's image and the words "Cora Youngblood Corson Day; June 3, 1915; Oklahoma State Building." Many telegrams of congratulation came from across the country. For example, the mayor of Tulsa sent the message "The city of Tulsa sends congratulations. Today's event is a well-deserved recognition of Oklahoma's most talented daughter."[79]

The next day, June 4, the C. G. Conn company also celebrated Cora

Cora Youngblood Corson Day with the 101 Ranch. June 1915.
Courtesy of the Museum of Tulsa History.

Youngblood Corson Day at its exhibition in the Fine Arts Building.[80] This was a significant endorsement as the other big name associated with Cora's by C. G. Conn was John Philip Sousa, who gave a performance later that month, on June 28. Reflecting the significance of Cora's name, the *Music Trade Review* reported on Sousa's planned engagement and followed by stating, "About the middle of the month this exhibit will also be well advertised, as arrangements have been made to have Cora Youngblood Corson's girl musicians play there."[81] This great honor cemented Cora's legacy as a representative of Oklahoma and placed her Native persona in a new light. She became nationally associated with and celebrated by Oklahoma. In the public's eyes, Cora represented every part of Oklahoma; she was a cowgirl, a Native, a settler, a woman, and a musician.

Once the performance ended in July, Cora took her group back to her ranch in Oklahoma for a break, which lasted from July and into August. While in Anadarko, the group decided to "regale their home folks with their high-

Empress Theatre, Tulsa, Oklahoma.
Author's collection.

class musical entertainment."[82] Unsurprisingly, this show sold out and "the girls who made Anadarko famous" could not fit any more spectators into the opera house.[83] During this period, the group changed its name to Cora Youngblood Corson and Her Oklahoma Musical Maidens, despite several of the women being from out of state.

After a rest in Anadarko, the group traveled to Tulsa to perform at the Empress Theatre for four days.[84] On August 3, Cora and the women performed for the Tulsa Chamber of Commerce at a luncheon at the Hotel Tulsa. After their performance, Edward O. Tilbourne, secretary of the organization, announced that "they played their brass instruments better than any feminine organization he had ever heard and mentioned the fact that the Chamber of Commerce appreciated the 'boosting' that had been done for Oklahoma and Tulsa by Miss Corson in all parts of North America."[85] The recognition of Cora's role in promoting Oklahoma on the national and international stage confirmed her ability to represent the state and its cultural heritage.

After their stay in Tulsa, the group performed at the Cozy Theatre in Okmulgee, Oklahoma. The small town enthusiastically announced the performance as "undoubtedly the greatest and most expensive vaudeville act ever brought to Okmulgee."[86] The group performed in Okmulgee for four days with constantly sold-out shows.[87] The sustained success of the show led one reporter to pose the question of forming an all-Oklahoma vaudeville bill:

> Why don't some enterprising person frame up an "All-Oklahoma" "vodvil" bill? Cora Youngblood Corson and her nine musical maids would be a good feature for such layout, Lucille Mulhal and her west offering would be available. Then there is the great "male single," "Oklahoma Bob" Albright, whose home is at Nowata and who is now a headliner on the Pantages time. Will Rogers, the greatest cowboy monologist and rope spinner on the stage today, lives at Claremore. Rogers was recently featured on the bill at the Palace, New York, over Trixie Friganza. There are any number of other "vodvil" stars—real ones too—who claim Oklahoma as their home. An all-star Oklahoma bill could be routed over some of the leading cities of the state—"mop up" is right![88]

This became the first mention of Cora alongside Will Rogers, whose career had just begun to take off. Unfortunately, this grand idea never came to fruition.

Beginning on August 25, 1915, the band dedicated itself to the fair circuit as a Fred M. Barnes attraction, performing at state fairs in Iowa, Wisconsin, Kansas, Oklahoma, and Texas.[89] After their final fair performance in October, the group saw a wonderful opportunity to advertise its appeal. In the November 13, 1915, edition of the *Billboard,* a large advertisement displayed the eight fairs played by Cora Youngblood Corson's Instrumentalists. It then told the reader, "If you want to know the value of the act, ask the Secretary of Fairs we have played for, not the men that are selling you acts."[90]

The year 1915 had cemented Cora and her act on both the vaudeville stage and the state fair grandstand, both coveted venues. The significance of her accomplishments landed Cora back on the cover of the *Billboard* on November 20, 1915. True to her nature, Cora did not slow down but immediately took the show on the road and returned to the vaudeville stage.

After these performances, the group traveled to Chicago, where the members spent Christmas at the Hotel Van Buren. However, this moment of joy and happiness, this feeling of being at the height of their career and being extraordinarily successful, would not follow the group into the new year. Immediately into 1916, Cora would find herself fighting not just for her reputation but also for the various workers in theaters.

FOUR

WAR AT HOME

Before 1915, Cora was associated with high vaudeville, which included popular and classical musicians; low vaudeville typically had more crass acts and came with a lower admission fee. She had built her public persona from that of a settler on the Plains to a celebrity whose shows routinely ran over $10,000 in production costs, which would be equivalent to more than $320,000 today. She performed with a gem-encrusted euphonium, and the women in her group all wielded golden instruments. Her performances exemplified class and elegance at a level few could afford to attend, and she certainly would not be seen in small local theaters. However, by the end of 1915, Cora found herself in conflict with the Vaudeville Managers Protective Association (VMPA), a powerful organization of major theater owners.

Within vaudeville, the major theater chains fell under two cartels of theater managers. The Vaudeville Managers Association (VMA) was dominated by the Keith-Albee chain, which controlled major theaters throughout the United States and Canada. In Chicago and most of the West, the Orpheum circuit dominated through the Western Vaudeville Managers Association (WVMA). To assist in acquiring acts for its theaters, the VMA created the United Booking Office (UBO) in 1907, a theatrical employment agency that allowed all the theaters to book acts that had previously been unavailable to certain venues. It also ended the bidding wars among managers for popular acts.[1]

This seemed to be advantageous to both the actors and theaters, but the VMA soon became a monopsony in which this single employer dominated the labor market. The theater managers could control the pay and conditions of their acts. This issue only increased in 1913, when Edward Albee II managed to gain effective control over both the VMA and WVMA, essentially controlling most of the acts in the country. This meant that the Keith-Albee chain controlled most of the theaters and booking and thus could enforce any rule regarding pay for its acts. The acts that paid their dues had access to the best theaters and schedules, but this became a source of contention for many acts. These unions held ultimate power over most of vaudeville, removing any control from the artists who wanted to perform in the larger theaters. Those who did not toe the line would find themselves unable to secure bookings and therefore could not make a living in theater.

In response, actors quickly banded together to form the White Rats Actors' Union, the first union for vaudeville artists in the United States. They chose the name as a nod to one of the founding members, Mark Murphy, who had prematurely snow-white hair. They also noted that "rats" spelled backwards is "star."[2] The organization only accepted white male members into its ranks, but in 1910 it received a charter from the American Federation of Labor and founded the Associated Actresses of America as a sister organization to allow the membership of women.[3]

Despite the union's efforts, by 1915, Keith-Albee used the UBO to increase its reach into almost 1,500 theaters.[4] It steadily increased its pressure on acts for more fees and more control over their performances. If an act did not follow Keith-Albee's rules, it would be placed on a blacklist and barred from all major theaters under the control of the VMA or WVMA.

Cora Youngblood Corson's popularity in 1914 had propelled her into the largest theaters in the country, with record attendance. Because of her success, she could negotiate a better deal for her act, against the VMA's wishes. She began pushing back on January 4, 1916, by announcing that she would not pay the VMA "a booking fee equal to half her salary or more." However, the VMA did not take kindly to her demands. It refused to give her performance time on one of the large western circuits it controlled. On top of this, Cora was placed firmly on the blacklist to ensure that she would no longer be able to perform at any of the major theaters she had once graced.[5]

Instead of backing down, Cora decided to fight back against the VMA, VMPA, and UBO, which she called "the trust," by calling upon the support of her native state. Fortunately, her farm in Anadarko brought in around $10,000 a year, which allowed her the freedom to openly confront the VMPA without much damage to her livelihood.[6] Her reputation as the "Oklahoma Girl," and internationally as "the world's most versatile lady musician," meant that her opinion held weight in the field of vaudeville. However, she had been popular in the theaters considered "high vaudeville," which meant she was typically out of touch with the working class that would attend any small-town theater. To succeed in Oklahoma, she needed to reinvent her image to appeal to the public that normally had not been able to afford or travel to see her performances.

To accomplish this, she presented herself as an independent artist and proud Oklahoman. She told the papers:

> My first move will be to invade my home state, where everybody believes in fair play. I shall take my act, with scenery, costumes, gold instruments, and all other properties, into the theaters of Oklahoma that are not controlled by these disreputable, bloodsucking Chicago grafters, and show them that I can prove my case before the greatest court in the world—the American public. The trust figures that its word is law—that it is the supreme court of vaudeville—but I know better. I know that they cannot survive if they do not give the theater patrons their money's worth. Dozens of good acts are laying off now, while cheaper ones are working, but I am not going to lay off. I am going to keep working. I leave for Oklahoma tonight, and I shall play the large towns and the small ones. The trust evidently wants a fight. They shall have it.[7]

True to her words, Cora immediately made her way to Oklahoma.

Once home, Cora began a "tour of two months throughout her native state," much to the benefit of small-town theaters that had never seen such high-quality vaudeville. Of course, the towns had the VMPA to thank for their good luck, and they made sure to mention it in their advertisements.

Cora Youngblood Corson's Instrumentalists in Vinita, Oklahoma. January 23, 1916. Author's collection.

In Claremore, Oklahoma, the paper announced that she had arrived due to "fighting the vaudeville trust." The paper also mentioned that the trust had "blacklisted Miss Corson because she played a theatre in Chicago that was not on their list." Fortunately, Cora's fighting spirit led her to "show them that she can 'get by' without their assistance." The paper also said that everyone should see the show because there was no question it would be "the greatest vaudeville attraction ever booked to appear in Claremore."[8]

The women upheld their reputation in every theater they graced in Oklahoma and Kansas. In Tahlequah, Oklahoma, the paper lamented that "the only objection heard being that it was over too soon," but if they returned "they will be met by a large audience."[9] In Vinita, Oklahoma, the act was declared "one of the best attractions seen."[10] Coffeyville, Kansas, echoed this, stating that the act would be "the best vaudeville act ever playing Coffeyville."[11] In Collinsville, Oklahoma, the paper said that the town "is to be treated to the best show obtainable in this part of the country . . . No act of higher class and no troupe with more native talent and with wider popularity could have been booked in Collinsville than Cora Youngblood Corson and her ladies' concert band." It also mentioned that "it is the act which the state of Oklahoma unanimously selects to represent it in theatrical circles everywhere."[12]

The Collinsville paper also remarked that "Cora is now waging a war with the vaudeville trust, and with the support of the Oklahoma constituency is making enormous headway in the fight." Her reputation became the novelty to sell the act: "This is the smallest town the act has ever shown in, having played in every town of any consequence in America. They have been featured at World expositions and exploited at state fairs everywhere they ever went and have painted the name of Oklahoma in conspicuous lights all over the United States."[13] Throughout the year, the group continued to perform at smaller theaters throughout the state while speaking out against the unfair policies of major theater managers.

In a move to force the VMPA into an agreement with the White Rats, in January 1916 Cora attempted to get a law passed in Oklahoma to ensure that the White Rats Actors' Union would be the main organization for vaudeville performers. She began a campaign "among local lawmakers and labor union representatives on behalf of a bill that would require all vaudeville acts playing theaters in this state to have a White Rats Actors' Union contract with the manager of the house they play." It was an odd twist. Despite arguing that she fought against monopolistic organizations, she ultimately attempted to create one herself with the White Rats at the helm. As one of the lifetime members of the Associated Actresses of America, and being independently wealthy, she could put up this fight without fear. However, other acts were not so fortunate and could not afford to go against the wishes of the major theaters. The *Tulsa Daily World* reported that it was "understood that state federation of labor will approve her bill and that there will be little opposition to the passage of the act."[14] However, the bill seems not to have passed. This perhaps shows that Cora was less concerned with the practices of the VMPA than with the restriction on her career. To maintain control of her popularity, Cora had simply changed her act. Now she had to change the laws to retain her career in vaudeville.

The blacklist left Cora with few options to get her voice out to the public and fellow performers. She found an avenue in the *Billboard,* but so too did her opponents. The magazine became a public battleground between not only Cora but also, by extension, the White Rats Actors' Union against the VMPA. Major James Doyle and Harry De Veaux, two vaudeville performers who did not agree with the tactics or leadership of the White Rats, first wrote to the *Billboard* to attack Harry Mountford, the leader of the White Rats, for his failure in leadership and the past failings of the union.

In response, Cora penned her first column, in which she established her position and arguments against the VMPA, giving the "other side" of the case:

> Dear Sir,
>
> This is a letter from a woman.
>
> This is a letter from a performer.
>
> This is a letter from a member of the Associated Actresses of America.
>
> This is a letter on behalf of the White Rats Actors' Union.

Cora then proceeded to refute the arguments made by Doyle and De Veaux, declaring that "neither of this pair is sincere, and . . . they could be of no benefit to any organization of performers. They are traitors." Cora then argued that the *Billboard* had turned against the actors in support of the VMPA, which she claimed had paid off the major vaudeville publications. Her mistrust of the paper had precedent as *Variety* had openly dismissed the White Rats and would not run their articles. Cora saw this as the beginning of a new fight, against the very publications that had once used her image on the covers of their magazines. She pointedly argued, "If it is to be the performer versus the theatrical trust and *The Billboard* let us know it!"[15] This open letter began Cora's very public support of the White Rats Actors' Union. Unfortunately, Cora's rush into openly attacking the largest vaudeville publications at the time meant that she would also lose her best avenue for widespread public relations. Without the magazines, she would no longer have a national reputation, further reducing her ability to control her public image.

The VMPA had managed to push her into a small corner, but Cora refused to back down. Instead, she doubled down on her support of Oklahoma as a state that believed in fair practice. It appears that Cora saw Oklahoma as an area where she could control the narrative while keeping her career alive. To accomplish this, Cora continued to proclaim her love for the state of Oklahoma as she continued her fight:

> The people of Oklahoma have always given me their unsolicited support. They have stood by me from the time I started in the music business and their encouragement has made me what I am, the most widely known lady musician in North America. I, in turn, have spelled my native state O-K-L-A-H-O-M-A in capital letters wherever I have appeared. And I am sure that in my present fight against the vaudeville trust they are going to stand by the girl who is engaged in the fight of her life. This battle is not waged selfishly, but on behalf of hundreds of other girls in the profession who are being placed under the contemptible ban of the trust's blacklist.
>
> Should I win this fight I will have Oklahoma to thank for my success, and Oklahoma will, in turn, be enabled to point with pride to their girl, the first professional woman to oppose the vipers who are attempting to dictate to all the theatrical world. It's a big battle, but it's being fought by a big girl with the assistance of the people of her native state. Oklahomans have overcome big odds in building this glorious commonwealth. They do not know the meaning of the word "quitter." I learned that during my residence in this state, and that is why I am doing what I am.
>
> I was brought up in Oklahoma and was taught to believe that we were free to do as we please so long as we did not violate the laws of the commonwealth. I did not believe that any body of men could make laws of their own that would forbid me making an honorable living in my chosen profession. And with that in mind I have taken it upon myself to place myself in your hands.
>
> Musically yours,
> Cora Youngblood Corson
> Of and For Oklahoma[16]

Cora's passionate plea to her state came before a performance at Busby Theater in McAlester, Oklahoma. This letter showcased not only her love for the state but also her belief that Oklahomans would support a grassroots effort to fight against the trust. Her performances in small towns did not threaten the VMPA economically, but it did deny them the ability to completely control Cora's stage career.

As the group continued to perform across the state, the members' musical ability became the draw. For instance, the Overholser Opera House in Oklahoma City, considered the best theater in the city, had the group perform. This endorsement by the Overholser drew attention, such as from the *Kingfisher Times,* which stated that the band's booking there "in itself ought to be guarantee enough that it is a high-class company."[17]

Cora continued to use these opportunities to create public sympathy for her cause by writing directly to the people of Oklahoma. She wrote of her dislike for press agents and said that she only cared for the people and their happiness:

> The happiest day of my life was when I appeared at the Panama Exposition on Oklahoma Day. I have had many pleasant days in my life, but the one the State of Oklahoma gave me there stands foremost in my memory. It was not the expression of one or two people, but a handshake from all the people of a splendid commonwealth.
>
> My heart was in my mouth, tears stood in my eyes on that occasion which will ever be dear in my memory. It seemed to me that all of Oklahoma was there, proud of a native girl who had made good, glad in her success and glad of the opportunity to show it.
>
> I mean to show the people of Oklahoma that Oklahoma grit coupled with Oklahoma indorsement is a combination which nothing but the greatest of success can reward.[18]

Cora wanted to ensure that the people of Oklahoma knew where her heart lay, and that her fight could succeed with their support.

In April 1916, the Southwest Vaudeville Managers Association added a new circuit in Missouri, Oklahoma, and Texas. Acts for this route were booked by Charles E. Hodkins out of the Pantages offices in Chicago. Since they did not have an affiliation with the UBO or VMA, Cora and her group managed to secure booking to head a show on the circuit and proved to be a big feature.[19] With the managers association, they toured through Oklahoma and Texas until May.

During this time, Cora performed on the euphonium, tuba, and bagpipes at the twenty-fifth annual convention of the Oklahoma Press Association.[20] Following this performance, which capped a "very-successful season," Cora took a well-deserved rest in Anadarko until July.[21] During this break, the White Rats Actors' Union appointed Cora as deputy organizer for the state of Oklahoma, making her the first woman in a leadership position in the union. This was the break that Cora had been building toward with her campaigns through Oklahoma. By securing a local leadership position, she could now take the next steps to return to the national stage. Cora took this mantle and began a "red hot campaign" for the White Rats. She campaigned for theaters to combat the UBO by booking only White Rats members. In Tulsa, she succeeded, when the Broadway theater, which marked the start of the southwest circuit, adopted the closed shop policy of White Rats, meaning it would only hire acts that belonged to the union.[22] This small victory within Oklahoma opened the possibility of sparking change nationwide.

In July, members of the musician's union in Oklahoma City allied themselves with the stagehands and movie operators to walk out in protest, seeking higher wages. Since Cora now led the White Rats of Oklahoma, she joined the strike until the demands of the strikers were met. The managers of the theaters held firm and attempted to hire other acts. However, Cora argued that the theaters would be "unable to secure other performers to fill in until there is a settlement of the controversy."[23] These strikes garnered national news as part of a larger fight against the VMPA, giving Cora a not-so-glamorous return to a national spotlight.

On July 16, stage employees from the Folly, Liberty, and Lyric theaters in Oklahoma City walked out alongside some motion picture operators, demanding a raise of three dollars a week. The theater managers declared that they would simply hire new employees or "go behind the scenes and in the booths to keep the shows running" themselves.[24] A week into the strike, no ground had been gained for either side. The Lyric theater, under the management of Peter Sinopoulo, continued to show five acts and claimed that he could hold out against these strikes.[25] On July 28, the strike escalated, with a picket line forming that impeded the approach to each theater.[26] The picket began showing signs of success, and some acts began to abandon their contracts. However, the theater managers began to argue that the acts had quit due to threats of violence from the strikers.[27]

Cora in front of a White Rats theater
during the Oklahoma strikes. 1916.
Author's collection.

After two weeks, the strike escalated once again as libelous statements began appearing in the newspaper from the managers of the Lyric, Liberty, and Folly theaters. The Tucker Brothers, owners and publishers of the *Free Pointer* newspaper, worked with the managers of the Metropolitan and Dreamland theaters to bring a $25,000 lawsuit against the picketed theater owners led by Sinopoulo. Cora also announced that a strike of the stagehands in Tulsa would be likely to put more pressure on theater managers in the state.[28] To this end, W. M. Smith, manager of the Empress Theatre in Tulsa, told the newspaper that the White Rats wanted the impossible: that he should hire only union-associated acts. He argued that the fight should be between the booking agents in Chicago and the White Rats, rather than targeting the theater managers directly.[29]

To promote their own acts, the White Rats and leaders from the other unions raised money to rent the Metropolitan Theatre in Oklahoma City and provide an alternative venue for customers who wanted to support the strikers. Not only was Cora instrumental in acquiring the lease but she and her band also paraded through Oklahoma City to announce that they would be performing at the Metropolitan with nine other vaudeville acts. Although the venue was used by all the striking unions, the White Rats bore the brunt of the cost for the lease.[30] Unfortunately, the theater could not operate at a profit, and it drained so much money from the White Rats that the organization had to borrow money to continue its activities.[31]

As the strike continued, public opinion began to favor the strikers. The theaters in Oklahoma City started seeing far fewer in attendance on an average night. The unions began declaring their victory over the Oklahoma City Theatrical Managers' Association.[32] However, an ultimate victory still looked out of reach as both sides declared "they have plenty of money to back them and are supremely confident of winning." Ultimately, the strike would end with either the theaters being blacklisted by the White Rats or the Rats being destroyed as an organization.[33] Furthermore, this crusade was not supported by all White Rats, and some saw Cora's strike as a ridiculous request. Dr. Joy's Sanitarium, an act that also belonged to the White Rats, denounced Cora and the strike, writing, "Miss Cora Youngblood Corson, who lives in Oklahoma City or neighborhood, and who had nothing to lose, thought she'd call a strike because a couple of stagehands wanted $3 a week more, and I should pull out and lose a few hundred. I think it's unfair to acts that come down there."[34]

The strike also created a poor image of Oklahoma in the press, meaning Cora was losing the war of public perception. One article stated that people feared traveling to the state because of the troubles: "Such things do not help the reputation of any city and especially one in the southwest. People from the east are all under the impression that Oklahoma is populated by bandits, cowboys, and wild Indians, with bandits in the majority. Some of them are reluctant to come to the state in times of peace and it is a wonder that they will come at all when a theatrical war is raging."[35]

Nevertheless, undaunted, Cora and her Rats continued the strike. Cora also took the fight to the courts, suing the Theatrical Managers' Association for $20,000 after an article published by the association reflected poorly on her.[36] In contrast, Harry Mountford, the president of the White Rats Actors' Union, praised Cora and the strike in *Variety* magazine:

> Miss Corson is in this fight and accepted the position of Honorary Chief Deputy Organizer for Oklahoma because she felt that she could do some good for the men and women among whom she has spent many years, and with whom she earns her living. Her actions and attitude in this matter have proved her an honest, fearless, unselfish, and generous-hearted woman—and the first reward that she received from the scurrilous and libelous pens of the suborned newspapers is that she is doing this for pay.[37]

In August, new pickets began to form in front of the Empress Theater in Tulsa as the Oklahoma strikes grew. On August 22, the tension escalated as two men were arrested while picketing the Empress. Officially, they were arrested for disturbing the peace—by talking during their pickets. The White Rats promised to fight this arrest up to the highest courts.[38] Despite the union support, both men were fined twenty-five dollars.[39] This incident further widened the divide between the cities, the theater managers, and the labor union, so much so that the Oklahoma State Federation of Labor pass a resolution denouncing the actions of J. H. McEwen, president of the Tulsa Chamber of Commerce.[40] For Cora, it seems, these strikes succeeded as a publicity stunt, giving her more control to expand out of Oklahoma. During the strike, Cora and her group took a break from Oklahoma to travel to St. Louis and begin a performance tour, leaving the strike to continue without her leadership.[41] This appears to show that Cora's leadership was not the goal in pushing the strike; instead, Cora used the White Rats Actors' Union and its resources to regain control of her image.

Without Cora's leadership, and with the poor publicity, the strike soon lost steam. The introduction of the White Rats brought too many issues to the cause. Cora and her Rats demanded a "closed shop" policy under which only union-associated acts could perform at the theaters. This absurd demand damaged the public image of the stagehands' plight. By September, the *Employer*, the journal of the Oklahoma Employers Association, declared that the strike had "fizzled out. It has been a fizzle from the beginning."[42] That same week, more arrests and fines were handed to picketers in Oklahoma City.[43]

Perhaps to save their image, the White Rats began to argue that they had planned a nationwide strike in October, but the Oklahoma strikes provided a good starting point for them. Francis Gilmore, an organizer for the White Rats, told the press that the heart of the issue was the theatrical trust "composed of the Interstate and Orpheum Circuits, Western Manager association, and United Booking association." The Rats had three purposes for their strikes: "to eliminate graft by booking agents; enforcement of closed shop policy for White Rats only; protection of women of the profession against unscrupulous booking agents and managers."[44] Cora's support and small successes in Oklahoma proved that they could fight back if they had the support of the public, but it also showed that Cora could use these strikes as a way to return to national attention.

On September 16, the idea that an Oklahoma State Board of Arbitration and Conciliation should be formed gained traction, and by September 23 the newly formed board investigated the strike.[45] After testimony from all parties, the board suggested a compromise that would include a contract between managers and stagehands that only union stage employees would be employed in the city; that wages would be increased by three dollars per week; that workers would not have to arrive before 11:00 a.m., would be given proper time for relief periods, lunch, and supper, and would not be required to work later than 10:30 p.m.; and that all those who went on strike would be reinstated in their positions with the theaters. This decision did not include any discussion of the White Rats' demand to hire only their performers.[46]

The theater managers chose not to follow these recommendations and instead increased their opposition to the strikers. On October 14, the Oklahoma City commissioners, working with the theater managers, passed an ordinance that made it "unlawful for any person, or persons, to walk, stand, or loiter on any street, sidewalk, alley, or public place within the city of Oklahoma City, in front of, or near to any place of business, and call out, speak to, or attract the attention of any person along such street, sidewalk, alley or public place, with the intent to induce such person or patronize or not to patronize such place of business." The ordinance also made it illegal to display a sign or banner while walking or standing on any street.[47]

In response, the pickets began again, with Mayor Edward Overholser declaring he would not enforce the ordinance until he had "looked over the situation."[48] Meanwhile, the ordinance went before the high court to determine its constitutionality.[49] Soon, another blow came down upon the White Rats. On November 1, 1916, the Vaudeville Managers Protective Association placed a national order against booking any White Rats acts because of the union's picketing activities in Oklahoma.[50] On top of this, E. F. Albee founded the National Vaudeville Artists in 1916 as a "company union" for vaudeville artists, in order to take away the strength of the White Rats.[51] Membership in this organization became a requirement for artists to book with the UBO, which caused even more acts to leave the White Rats Actors' Union. This blow and the continuance of the strike dwindled support for the strike, and the White Rats began to distance themselves from an active role in Oklahoma City.[52] The strike had damaged the union's national image and had shaken the faith of many union members, who began to call out Harry Mountford's shady dealings and hypocritical attitude toward striking union members.[53] The strike seemed to be the beginning of the end for the union.

On the other hand, November brought some success for both Cora and her family as she recovered from the stress of performing and leading the Oklahoma strikes. Cora's brother-in-law, Glenn Condon, began his campaign for state representative. Cora and her band performed as entertainment for his rallies in Broken Arrow, Sand Springs, and Skiatook.[54] Meanwhile, Harry Mountford used Cora's Oklahoma strike to push the case for the White Rats to be acknowledged by the Federation of Labor, instead of a new union, the Actor's Equity Association. The White Rats' cooperation with the various union stagehands, musicians, and operators in Oklahoma City and Tulsa became the key feature in Mountford's argument as he extolled Cora's successful leadership.[55]

During this period, the editors of both the *Billboard* and *Variety* began to voice their opinions against the White Rats, and specifically against Cora Youngblood Corson. The editors of the *Billboard* announced that they would print pro–White Rats letters but they did not support the union. Cora had lost the war of public relations. The push against the *Billboard* and *Variety* had caused the loss of the only hope she had of reaching the national public eye as she had done in years prior. The *Billboard* stated, "We are convinced that the White Rats Actors' Union is not what it purports to be—that it is not a union at all, but an organized predatory raid upon the resources of the vaudeartists of America." This opinion meant that the magazine would not print any pro-Rats advertisements from Harry Mountford.[56] The White Rats would not receive any support from the *Billboard* for their crusade. Likewise, in an article titled "Cora's Self Boosting," *Variety* criticized Cora for sending to acts performing at nonunion theaters letters that contained "much literature mostly about the Cora Youngblood Corson act."[57] Despite negative national attention, Cora continued to sell out the small Oklahoma theaters before moving into Kansas at the end of November.

In December 1916, Cora took her band through Kansas. The newspapers heralded the group's talents, enticing all to come watch the special show that previously could only be seen in major theaters. The *Columbus Daily Advocate* also wrote an article detailing the accolades of Cora Youngblood Corson from "notable men of the country." Many of these had been printed in various newspapers over the previous months, a repetition that may indicate an attempt to salvage parts of Cora's reputation that may have been damaged through the Oklahoma strikes. It read, in part:

> "Someday this little girl will be greater in her line than Sousa."—interpreted from an expression by the late Apache Warrior, Geronimo, who presented Miss Corson with a tree woven blanket shortly before his death.—Anadarko, Okla., Sept. 12th, 1908
>
> "Such music can only be inspired by genius."—Wm. H. Taft, Cincinnati, Ohio, Notification Day
>
> "Thank God that Oklahoma has produced a girl who can play like you, Miss Corson."—The late Wm. McKinley, at Buffalo World's Fair
>
> "If you are as beautiful in looks as the music you play is good, you must be the prettiest young lady in the universe."—Thomas Pryor Gore, Senator from Okla., Anadarko, Okla.

"It is greater to be a silver-toned Musician like Miss Corson than to be a silver-tongued orator."—Wm. J. Bryan, Anadarko, Okla., Oct. 2nd, 1902[58]

As she had done in the past, Cora attempted to draw a connection to Geronimo and connect back to her Native exoticism. However, these statements are so ludicrous that they show a desperate attempt to regain a positive image. For instance, Cora did not play at the Buffalo World's Fair and there is no reference to William J. Bryan ever mentioning Cora during his visit to Anadarko.

The women continued their tour through the Midwest as a traveling Orpheum special show. The band also continued, under the moniker "Oklahoma's Prodigys."[59] Cora's success as an independent show continued to draw the ire of the VMPA. If a theater booked Cora's act, it received a letter from the VMPA to convince it to stop booking independently and instead to use the trust to obtain "a good consistent show each week."[60] Cora had successfully made her way out of Oklahoma and into more theaters against the power of the VMPA. Her successful use of Oklahoma to change her public image allowed her some power to control her own career without the theater managers. However, her good tidings and the successful press would not last against the power of the theater monopolies.

In February 1917, J. Leslie Spahn arrived in Chicago, Illinois, ahead of the act, having booked it in advance. But Chicago was a powder keg for the White Rats Actors' Union. The union had reportedly planned a strike in the first week of February, but it failed to materialize in Chicago. The vaudeville managers did not even take precautions against it as they paid little attention to strike rumors. In response and to save face, Mountford announced that the New York headquarters' call for a strike had not been authorized. Mountford also declared that the "acts of the V.M.P.A. are in direct contradiction of the Sherman Anti-Trust Law" and that he and "W. Rubin, a Milwaukee labor attorney," and "Edw. Nockels, secretary of the Chicago Federation of Labor," had met with U.S. District Attorney Charles Clyne to ask for prosecution of the vaudeville managers.[61] This trouble would soon boil over and make Cora national news once more.

On March 8, 1917, the White Rats called for a strike of Chicago theaters. Although the union expected more support, only one act, the Four Danubes, walked out. Many theaters had no problems and continued to run smoothly. However, the Academy, Hippodrome, Kedzie, Lincoln, and Windsor theaters had pickets working in front of their establishments, with strikers distributing handbills and declaiming the unfair work conditions.[62] Cora took up the mantle for the White Rats, and as head of the Associated Actresses of America she led a spirited campaign on "behalf of unionism for actors and actresses via booklets and folders."[63]

Cora, along with Grace and Hattie Acton, Gladys Cronk, Ethel Hiatt, Mae McBride, and Ida Mundell, joined the picketers at various theaters. On March 8, Cora and her band picketed the Lincoln Theatre, where they were arrested and "taken to the Sheffield Station and later released on bonds." On the eleventh, Cora and a few members of her band were once again arrested, for picketing the Kedzie alongside other strikers.[64] That same evening, six more of Cora's band were arrested while picketing the Windsor, for "creating a plot and disturbing the peace."[65] The White Rats claimed that there would be a larger tie-up in Chicago within two weeks that would result in a big victory for them.[66] However, such a victory did not materialize.

Instead, this "nationwide strike" failed spectacularly, with reportedly only twenty acts following the order. The *Billboard* declared the strike "the most dismal of failures, and even the most sanguine of the Rat supporters are fast beginning to realize the hopelessness of their cause." No theaters suffered any loss of shows or business. To the editors of the *Billboard,* the strike seemed a "last dying effort" of the leadership that had failed to accomplish any major victories for their union. The "rodent organization" could not wield its membership as an effective weapon against the VMPA, and now the nation had witnessed its failure. In response, many of the theater managers asserted that they would no longer hire acts belonging to the White Rats. Marcus Loew of the Loew circuit publicly announced that "so long as I am in the show business none of them will ever work for me, you can depend upon that."[67]

The strike lost even more power when the law turned against the strikers. On March 14, 1917, Chicago's Judge Jesse A. Baldwin issued an injunction against several leaders of the White Rats Actors' Union. The injunction established a restraining order against many picketers, including Cora Youngblood Corson, "and all associations, firms, and persons assisting and aiding them or conspiring with them." The judge strictly commanded the strikers to "desist and refrain from interfering with said complainants, said theatres and business, respectively, and with any of the employees of the said theatres." This meant that they could not picket or even hand out union material in the vicinity of the theaters.[68] This concerned many of the Rats as a month previous the same judge had issued an antipicketing injunction against a garment worker's strike. He followed this by sentencing one of the striking workers to sixty days in Bridewell prison.[69]

On March 23, 1917, *Variety* published an article detailing how the blacklist worked. The list was designed so that "an agent running afoul of it will lose his booking franchise in whatever offices or agencies he may have the privilege of booking." The VMPA indicated that any agent booking a blacklisted act, even under an assumed name, would face consequences. Each agent had to research each act they booked to ensure that none of the actors or actresses had been placed on the list. The official list would not be published, but "any agent booking through any office of a circuit or manager belonging to the V.M.P.A. may be informed whether any names or titles are on the blacklist." The VMPA designed this to disenfranchise outside agents and essentially force out of vaudeville anyone who raised their ire.[70]

Unfortunately, Cora seemed to be placed at the top of this list, and the VMPA vehemently fought against her and her career. As an article in *Variety* put it, "While the White Rats troubles were on, Miss Corson had written and talked. She easily wrote and talked herself onto the Keith's 'blacklist' and Miss Corson liked it—she kept on working and kept on talking." Aid to the cause of the VMPA accidentally came from the White Rats leadership. In a public statement, Harry Mountford's frustrations came to the forefront. Due to the lack of success of the strikes in New York City and Boston, he claimed that "the Loew circuit for the past six weeks has been playing the lowest class of acts, made up of the sweepings of the gutter, as no decent act would accept time on the Loew circuit because of the terrible conditions on it." This statement did not bring any support to the Rats but instead further isolated them from most vaudeville performers by driving an even larger rift between union and nonunion acts. This, paired with the lackluster showing for the strikes, led *Variety* to declare this period to be "the death knell to Mountfordism."[71] The term "Mountfordism" had become an aspersing term for discussing the White Rats Actors' Union, which meant that the death of Mountford's leadership spelled the end of the White Rats.

The VMPA also turned its wrath to those who had assisted Cora Youngblood Corson, such as E. E. Meredith of Chicago. Meredith edited and published the *Missouri Breeze*, a leading vaudeville and theatrical publication.

Meredith had assisted Cora in obtaining bookings in Chicago despite the blacklist. J. Leslie Spahn also used the *Breeze* office as his headquarters while working with Cora and the White Rats during their strike. As punishment, the VMPA announced that it would not allow Meredith "the usual courtesy of the booking offices and theatres given newspapermen hereafter."[72] This further alienated Cora from her allies, who feared retribution from the VMPA.

As public opinion turned against the White Rats, so too did the representation of Cora turn in the papers. The *Billboard* wrote that Cora had been "the greatest agitator on picket duty before the injunction against picketing." The magazine noted that "together with her eight girls she picketed in front of different houses and was arrested several times" and also mentioned that picketing would be classed as a misdemeanor and could result in imprisonment.[73] In a more negative tone, *Variety* wrote, "Cora Youngblood Corson expects a Carnegie medal for riding the Chicago police patrol wagons."[74] What little control her success in Oklahoma had given her now meant nothing. Unfortunately, in the face of the power of the VMPA, Cora would not return to the grand stages of vaudeville, even if she changed her identity multiple times to be exotic.

Back in Oklahoma, however, the impact of the Oklahoma City strikes still rang true. The *Morning Tulsa Daily World* wrote of her role in Chicago and published an interview with her on the matter, in which she stated:

> To slightly paraphrase the old saw—"it will never get well if you picket"—would be to misrepresent my case. I had a terrible headache one evening last week and was in anything but a good humor when I went from my hotel to picket, and the open air and excitement drove my illness clear out of mind and I enjoyed the evening very much.
>
> Picketing is not so exciting here as it was in Oklahoma City, but then the strike is young yet. Another thing which I figure counts against the excitement is the fact that all the theaters in Oklahoma City are within four or five blocks of each other while in Chicago the affected houses are so far apart that a picket at one house knows nothing of what is going on at the others . . .
>
> These visits to the police station are becoming commonplace. The time there is getting dull, so the officers have studied our ways of amusement. They dug up an old cornet that some prisoner had left there, and my girls played it a little one night. We often have games of checkers to pass the time.

> The police officers appear very much interested in the Cora Youngblood Corson act and have promised to come to the Columbia the "last half" to see us.
>
> I wish to take this opportunity to say that I did not come to Chicago with any idea of starting a strike, tho I am glad to have had an opportunity of doing my bit in the fight. I had nothing more to so with the strike than anyone else. I followed the instruction of my superiors just like anyone else.[75]

The group's "popularity" in Chicago garnered quite a bit of attention from fellow Oklahomans. Cora refused to back down and even "had a copy of the injunction framed and is very proud of it." According to the *Daily World* article, an unnamed wealthy oil magnate of Okmulgee, Oklahoma, had been in Chicago and had read the articles about Cora and her arrests. He had met Cora multiple times before and "was anxious to assist the plucky girl," so he "placed thousands of dollars in cash at her disposal and prepared to remain in Chicago indefinitely so as to put up cash bonds for Miss Corson and her assistants as long as the police cared to arrest them." The financial support for Cora came only from those who knew her connection to Oklahoma. Without any major union support, the strike would fail.

Unbeknownst to Cora or any of the other White Rats, their entire fight against the VMPA would come to a screeching halt on April 6, 1917, when the United States declared war on Germany, thrusting the country into the Great War. On April 10, Mountford called off a planned strike by the White Rats, arguing that it was their "patriotic duty, with the nation at war, to refrain from striking as proof of their loyalty and patriotism."[76] Another blow to the White Rats came when Theresa Maridol, an actress and wife to the president of Chicago's local chapter of the union, passed away later in the month. Cora and several members of her band served as pallbearers for the funeral in Mt. Carmel, Illinois.[77] With her funeral, any further desire to push their fight in Chicago subsided.

To find work for his clients, J. Leslie Spahn created a White Rats roadshow that would present acts that belonged to the union, although he did not always advertise this association.[78] Seven other acts joined Cora Youngblood Corson on this tour. All belonged to either the White Rats Actors' Union or the Associated Actresses of America. In an echo of her tour of Oklahoma the previous year, newspapers reported on the circumstances that had led to Cora's act performing at small local theaters. In Princeton, Illinois, the paper stated that it was "only because of labor trouble between the booking agents and the members of the actors' and actresses' unions that a star of this kind is secured for Princeton. Under normal conditions an actress of her reputation and standing would be booked for weeks and even months ahead on the Orpheum circuit."[79] The unfortunate truth in this statement reflects the depths to which Cora had fallen because of her union work.

This show continued through Illinois, garnering the same type of attention. In Henry, Illinois, the paper stated, "Such a program as the one Tuesday evening is not often seen in large city theaters, and to be in a place so small as Henry it is a rare treat."[80] The performance of such high-quality acts cost only thirty-five to fifty cents.[81] This could not last financially, however, and by June the act had ended its tour. Cora and her band returned to their homes for an extended break from performing. Cora returned to Anadarko, visited friends around Tulsa, and attended family reunions.[82]

By September 1917, Cora decided that she had no power to compete with the trust. The failure of the White Rats strike, coupled with her lack of power after being blacklisted for more than a year, had left her with no options. In desperation, she reached out to Eugene V. Debs, asking for assistance in fighting the union. Debs had very public career as an American socialist, political activist, trade unionist, and Socialist Party candidate for president of the United States. He became one of the most well-known socialists in the country, especially in Oklahoma, where his union, the Industrial Workers of the World, had become prominent. In the 1910s, the Socialist Party had become one of the dominant organizations in the state, with almost 20 percent of Oklahomans supporting the party.

On September 5, 1917, however, Cora received the disappointing response, delivered by Debs's brother, Theodore, that no help would be forthcoming:

> Dear Comrade Corson,
>
> Your very kind letter of the 26th is received. Your words of personal kindness in reference to my brother are all too generous, but I beg you to believe that I am deeply touched, as he will be, by this beautiful tribute of your confidence and esteem. Coming from you, one who knows and understands the struggle of the workers, one who staunchly upholds principle against the most bitter opposition, sacrifices and suffers for conviction,—such words

from such a comrade will be as cheering as they are inspiring and appreciated for more than these poor words of mine can express . . .

In the work you are doing you have the comfort and satisfaction of knowing that you are in the right; that you are building for the future; that your efforts are not in vain; and that it will live to bless all the race long, long after the Booking Trust is dead and remembered—if at all—only for its infamy.[83]

On October 3, 1917, Cora sent another telegram to Debs. Cora lamented that upon her arrival in Rochester, New York, the VMPA "have ordered my work cancelled on account of my fight for my organization." She pleaded for help from Debs, stating, "If I let them get away with this I'll be forced to quit."[84] A response has not survived but it does not seem that Debs was able to offer any assistance. These pleas for help seemed to be Cora's last gasp of hope before her fight slipped away.

That same month, the VMPA made good on its promise to press their blacklist even further. Cora Youngblood Corson and Her Octette had contracts to perform in the Buffalo, Family, and Lyric theaters in Rochester, New York, for the first few weeks of October 1917. Despite these contracts, the managers of the Family and the Lyric, "both house members of the Vaudeville Managers' Protective Association, were informed they could not play the act." The managers were reportedly given an ultimatum: If they allowed Cora to perform, then they would lose their membership in the VMPA. Cora threatened legal action against these houses, but the managers were "apparently agreeable to it in preference to playing the turn." Cora had apparently been booked through an "outside agent" and therefore should never have been given a contract due to the blacklist. As a result, Cora was not allowed to perform at the theaters.[85]

In November, both Cora and the White Rats Actors' Union continued to face major public issues. Harry Mountford faced a court case in the New York Supreme Court, during which he admitted to illegal operations between the union and the White Rats Realty Company. This created even greater strain between the few remaining White Rats members and the organization and further villainized the union in the eyes of the public. Alongside this, in Providence, Rhode Island, it became known that an act called "Florence Livingstone and Her Oklahoma Prodigies" had been booked at Edward M. Fay's theater through the M. R. Sheedy Agency in New York. Inquiry revealed that Florence Livingston was Cora Youngblood Corson under an assumed name. Further investigation revealed that Cora had also appeared at the Colonial Theatre in Newport, Rhode Island, as the "Nine Broadway Musical Belles," as well as at the Academy in Lowell, Massachusetts, and then had performed in Haverhill, Massachusetts, with these theaters being "booked through John J. Quigley of Boston." None of these theaters had a connection with the VMPA, but the blacklist against her still stood strong in the eyes of the association. Therefore, the VMPA turned its attention to the managers that had booked her.[86]

Variety reported that one of the managers, Fay, had filed "an application for membership" in the VMPA but that it had not been decided upon. It was assumed that by playing Cora at his theater, Fay likely eliminated "that house from any further consideration for V.M.P.A. membership." The article also believed "an immediate adjustment of the Sheedy agency" would come "in so far as it relates to booking theatres belonging to" the VMPA. This would be accomplished by targeting the theaters that used Sheedy as a booking agency, namely the "Gordon Brothers' theatres in New England." *Variety* believed the VMPA would "call upon the Gordons to withdraw from its membership, if the Gordons continue playing Sheedy bookings."[87] The VMPA would pursue its war against Cora through any means necessary.

By November 16, 1917, Fay had consulted his attorney, August Dreyer, about action against the VMPA. Fay told *Variety* he was "oppressed through the activity of the Vaudeville Managers' Protective Association in pronouncing his theater on a 'blacklist.'" In response, he and other businessmen in Providence were taking steps to "prevent action of that sort in the future" but would not comment on what action would be taken.[88] The John Quigley Association also incurred the enmity of the VMPA, though it argued that booking acts under false names allowed them to be booked through other agencies in the future.[89] However, the damage had been done and Cora could not perform. The consequences of Cora's union work had now grown to attacks on any theater that allowed her to play. Since she could not find any major theaters to book her act, she returned to Anadarko.

Cora had seen the crushing the end of her career in vaudeville in 1916. Her fight for union rights against the Vaudeville Managers Protective Association secured her spot on a blacklist that would follow her for years. To combat this injustice, Cora had turned to Oklahoma as a place where her union work would be supported, given the state's socialist leanings. By taking advantage of the rise of socialism among the working class, Cora attempted to regain control of her career. The strikes she led in Oklahoma City and Tulsa quickly gained national attention and spurred other strikes by the White Rats Actors' Union in major cities, with Cora as a leading figure. However, this could not save her career from its decline.

FIVE

WAR ABROAD

By the end of 1916, Cora had reached the lowest point in her career. The failure of the White Rats and the steady decline of her popularity seemed unstoppable. However, entry of the United States into World War I provided a unique opportunity for her to save her reputation and career, just as it had a profound impact on the state of Oklahoma. By its conclusion, the state would be transformed politically, and Cora would be transformed socially. The outbreak of the war left many agriculturalists in the state reeling as the German blockade of the Atlantic Ocean closed off European markets. The American entry into the war, in 1917, also led to the passing of the Selective Service Act, which called for all men between the ages of twenty-one and thirty to register for military service. The response to the draft was disastrous.

In August 1917, an armed revolt of tenant farmers erupted in Oklahoma, triggered by opposition to the draft and the issue of low crop prices. Many of the outraged tenant farmers had joined Oklahoma's Socialist Party and sought change by marching on Washington, DC. The rebels began burning bridges and cutting telegraph lines until groups of armed local authorities stopped the revolt. A few men died in the altercations and more than four hundred were arrested. Due to the failure of the rebellion and the extreme public backlash, the Oklahoma Socialist Party disbanded.[1] The Green Corn Rebellion revealed the intense opposition to the war in the state. It also created a negative image of Oklahoma in the rest of the nation.

Fortunately for the state, the reopening of European markets in 1916 increased demand for Oklahoma agricultural goods and brought farmers prosperity. Unfortunately, the aftermath of the Green Corn Rebellion, a year later, sparked a backlash against war decriers in Oklahoma. The state that had epitomized antiwar sentiment quickly gave way to enthusiastic and sometimes violent patriotism. A sense of antiradicalism became the norm in the American psyche as the war ramped up. Ideas of being unpatriotic or disloyal became the talk of foolish "individuals contradicting the unified ideal, and the war, [who] faced intense stigmas of being unpatriotic and disloyal because they were perceived to be derailing the spotlight from the war effort." Moreover, the American ideal during the war years promoted "beliefs of national unity, strength, and cohesion."[2] Any contradiction of the mainstream just made these ideas even stronger throughout society.

For women, adherence to the gendered national discourse of American patriotism resulted in what Annessa Ann Babic calls "patriotic women." In *America's Changing Icons,* Babic argues that "home front mobilization, gendered politics like women receiving the vote, the advancement of women in the labor force, and promises of suburbia all played a role in changing the face and duty of the patriotic female." Women "who acted against the mainstream showed patriotism through protest. They acted for the larger good . . . [but] did not always fit the ideal." Volunteerism reflected the heart of the nation, but women in military service contradicted mainstream ideas about female roles. Throughout the war, women were supposed to support the war effort at home as "wives, mothers, daughters, wartime factory workers, field nurses, and women who fought for equality," though some women did push the boundaries of these "manufactured images, revealing the patriotic female to be a complex and continually changing metaphorical icon."[3]

No one woman fit the ideal. Instead, the patriotic female image evolved as different aspects of their service were highlighted in the American press. This provided a new opportunity for Cora Youngblood Corson to once again change public perception and increase her popularity. Cora exemplified the national change, using the war to reinvent herself from a troublemaking socialist unionist into a patriotic American veteran of the war.

As the war ramped up for the United States, many vaudeville performers joined the military to do their part. Theaters were thus lacking much of the male entertainment they had enjoyed in the past. Then, in late 1918, the influenza epidemic closed many theaters around the country, resulting in a decline in vaudeville's popularity. To stay in the public eye, theatrical managers put full force behind the war effort. For instance, A. Paul Keith and E. F. Albee, joint owners of the B. F. Keith vaudeville circuit, assigned their highest paid actors and actresses, such as magician Harry Houdini and Lillian Russell, to war work. Reportedly, Russell "secured more recruits for the United States Marine Corps than any other single agency and was rewarded with a decoration and the rank of Colonel." The Keith theaters also became a highly effective fundraising platform for liberty loans throughout the war. While some performers dutifully contributed to the war effort at home, many joined the military, and for this, "generous provision was made," with "their names being carried on the payrolls for a large percentage of their salaries."[4]

Due to the blacklist, Cora could not take part in this vaudevillian effort. Instead, she put her efforts into supporting the Red Cross and promoting war gardens. On July 31, 1917, Cora wrote a letter to Oklahoma's Governor Robert Williams complaining that "the Red Cross has fallen down awful" in dozens of Oklahoma counties. She offered that her brother-in-law Glenn Condon might be interested in helping Oklahoma "make a much better showing then it has done." She also sent a photograph of her plowing her war garden with the caption "I am Doing My Bit."[5] These small measures were repeated by many Americans across the country to relieve the stress on the nation's agricultural system.

Patriotism and personal needs justified Cora's desire to act for the greater good of the country and her reputation. Her concern with aiding in the war effort culminated in the decision to brave the submarine-infested waters of the Atlantic Ocean and travel to Europe to entertain the men in service. In July 1917, Cora Youngblood Corson's Instrumentalists secured a tour of the Moss Empire theaters and twenty independent halls throughout Great Britain with "A. Scranton" of Scranton's Variety Agency in Manchester, England. This leg of their trip would be booked for forty-two weeks.[6] The band had changed over the previous year, so the eight women who went overseas with Cora were Graycia Acton, Gladys Cronk, Clairette and Simone Hamel, Ethel and Olive Hiatt, Ida Mundell, and Lela Myers. The "Oklahoma prodigies" also sailed with their manager, J. Leslie Spahn, while Glenn Condon joined them as "press representative."[7]

Condon had another reason for accompanying the band, in addition to entertaining the soldiers. At twenty-five years old, Condon became the youngest member of the Oklahoma legislature. He also worked as the editor of the *Tulsa Daily World* newspaper. Shortly after his election, the war broke out and he lent his talents to the Oklahoma Council of Defense as state chairman of the Four-Minute Men, an organization of public speakers who could give impromptu patriotic speeches. With the announcement of Cora's overseas intention, the Oklahoma Council of Defense solicited Governor Robert L. Williams to appoint Condon a commissioner of Oklahoma and to send him overseas to obtain firsthand information about the war and "how best it [the council] can serve Uncle Sam."[8] Condon would not stay for the entirety of the band's time overseas.[9] The stage was set for the band members to return to the headlines and to save their careers as court proceedings in the United States stalled.

Spahn turned to the American Express Company to arrange overseas transportation, about four months before they intended to sail. He and all the women applied for passports around October 1917, planning to leave in December and arrive in England the first week of January. Ida Mundell wrote in her personal journal, "Everyone told us we could not get passports as the governments were not letting any women travel on the ocean on account of submarine dangers and the governments needing all the shipping space." Fortunately, they "did not have a bit of trouble getting passports."[10] To travel overseas, they used the Cunard Line, which changed their sailing date three different times due to submarine activity.

On December 17, 1917, they prepared to sail for England onboard the RMS *Orduna*. The ship carried only about forty other paying passengers in addition to the nine members of the band, with only four other women. Filling the rest of the ship were 1,500 American soldiers, mostly belonging to Aero Squadrons: the Eleventh, the Twentieth, the 117th, and the 135th. The ship left New York Harbor for Halifax, and for this leg of the trip the women remained on the deck, taking in the sights before having supper with officers from the Aero Squadrons. However, seasickness quickly took the appetites of many of the passengers.

On December 20, the ship pulled into Halifax, sailing through the destruction from the Halifax Explosion, which had occurred only two weeks prior. A French cargo ship carrying high explosives had collided with another vessel, resulting in a massive explosion and fire that devastated Halifax and killed more than 1,500 people. Ida Mundell recorded that they "could see the destruction caused by the ship explosion. It looked as though an earthquake and fire together had destroyed things. Several ships were sunk or lying on their sides upon the bank." While anchored in the harbor, the band gave a concert in the second-class lounge for many first- and second-class passengers. The next day, they sailed out of Halifax to join the convoy that would take them to England. The women performed "Over There" as they were leaving.

In the initial days of their voyage, all the passengers underwent lifeboat drills and had to constantly carry their life preservers due to the threat of German submarines. To pass the time, the women chatted with the officers or relaxed in steamer chairs on deck while the soldiers had calisthenics. In the evening, Cora and the band would give a concert for various audiences and Cora sang some solos. Along with their short concerts for the passengers, Cora and her band also performed in aid of "seaman charities," created for the benefit of sailors' widows and children. Some of the soldiers played piano and sang. A "Mr. Palmer" of the YMCA and Glenn Condon gave recitals. Cora and the women "filled all the last half of it. Some on first part of the program were sick so we made the largest part of the entertainment. Three of the women was too sick to be there." They gave two more charity concerts to officers and enlisted men.

A small printing press aboard the ship allowed them to sell programs for a dollar apiece. It also printed the most important news that the wireless operator received every few days. Glenn Condon took advantage of this opportunity and edited the onboard paper. A fellow Oklahoman, Second Lieutenant Claude A. Webb from Tipton, Oklahoma, wrote home to his family that "Glenn Condon of the Tulsa World was on the boat with me coming over. I don't know what he was coming over for, but he was with Cora Youngblood Corson and her troupe of vaudevillists."[11] His casual mention of the group shows reflects Cora's success in creating a popular image of herself in Oklahoma in years prior.

During this tumultuous journey, the musical world in England began to announce the band's arrival in the county. On December 27, 1917, the Cora

Youngblood Corson Octette graced the cover of the *Performer*, the official magazine of the Variety Artistes' Federation and the leading theatrical publication in Great Britain. It announced the group's opening performance dates and heralded its spectacular shows. In preparation, the women had rehearsed aboard the ship, but seasickness still plagued them and affected their ability to play. Nonetheless, they continued to make the best of their trip. In the evenings, the women joined the soldiers in the dining room to play cards and checkers and to drink.

The coast of Ireland came into view on December 30. That night, the women decided to have an all-night watch party. They turned cablegrams in to the wireless operator to send home as soon as they safely landed in the United Kingdom. By 8:30 a.m., the ship stopped rocking and the vibration from the engines ceased. They had arrived safely in Greenock Bay in Scotland. After arriving safely, they learned the truth about their voyage. The captain had received a message "to change his course for there was near two hundred submarines formed a blockade waiting for our convoy." Regardless of the actual number of submarines, the pilot ship had been sunk on its way to meet the convoy, resulting in nearly all men being lost except for the radio operator. The convoy ahead of Cora's lost four ships. Along with the women and the soldiers, the *Orduna* also "carried four million dollars' worth of treasury notes and two million dollars' worth of gun cotton," while another ship in the convoy "was loaded with aeroplanes and one with horses and cattle." Fortunately, Captain Thomas M. Taylor had a "reputation of knowing how to dodge the Subs" and therefore rerouted the convoy to Scotland rather than their original destination of Liverpool, England.

When they docked at Glasgow, the soldiers began to disembark. Cora and her band waited on the ship until the next day, when custom officers came aboard to check their papers and luggage. This wait resulted in their missing the train for Manchester, so they stayed another night on the ship. The next morning, the women told the crew goodbye and disembarked. They soon boarded a train to take them to Manchester. They arrived late at night and met their booking agent's stenographer at the station. The city was cloaked in darkness as all lights had been painted over to protect the citizens from German air raids. At the hotel, the women asked whether there was any food and received a lunch of "a thin piece of boiled ham, two thin pieces of war bread, and a cup of tea." Once in their rooms, they found no running water, no heat, and an extra cost to have a fire. To keep warm, they slept two to a bed. Their volunteer service would not be comfortable, but the women trudged on.

Their first week in England would be confined to Manchester as they got their official paperwork sorted. They all needed individual identity and ration books. They had to register at the police station in every town they stayed in and had to notify the police of their departure. To have some sort of national identity in this foreign land, Cora looked all over Manchester for American flags and finally found a few little ones in a bookstore. The women wore them on their coats. On January 4, 1918, J. Leslie Spahn returned from a trip to London with Glenn Condon. He brought Cora a gift from a British soldier, a bracelet made of metal taken from the first German airplane brought down near Canterbury, England, in November 1917. The soldier had been a stage manager in the United States at one time and knew the vaudeville world intimately.

On January 7, their lives began to get into a familiar routine. They arrived at the Palace Theatre in Chelsea for rehearsal around noon. Immediately, an issue arose: the women were "in low pitch while the orchestra was in high." Some of the slides for their instruments were in the hotel trunks and some in the theater trunks. Cora's tuba had no high-pitch slides because it was built in low pitch. This mix-up did not bode well for their first performance in England.

In the end, Ida believed they had "a bum show but got by—everything seemed to be against us." Fortunately, the theater manager, audience, and agents seemed to like the performance. Adding to their worry, Scranton had brought George Foster, "the most noted Variety Agent in the world," to see the act. But he commented that their act "was the most beautiful and the best dressed act that ever come over from America." His only criticisms were that the music was too slow and that they should put in two popular songs instead of so much classical music. On their way back to their boardinghouse, Spahn carried Cora's euphonium and case and rode on the top level of the bus. As he was coming down the stairs he slipped and fell into the street. The euphonium flew into the street, but the case saved it from any substantial damage. To avoid issues in later performances, Cora purchased a "high pitch bassoon tuba" the next day.

On January 11, the women performed at their first concert for wounded soldiers. The lord and lady mayor attended this performance, at the Central Library in Islington. J. P. Mitchelhill, manager of Collins Music Hall and organizer of the event, made a speech before Cora and her band performed, in which he told the audience that the group were Americans and had braved the submarines to get there. He also mentioned that these men were the first soldiers for whom they would play. Just before the women played "Over There," Glenn Condon said a few words about the song and told them how popular it was with American soldiers. This performance went well and established the group's reputation with the soldiers of the British and Canadian Expeditionary Forces.

On their way back to their rooms, the women noticed the searchlights placed strategically around the city. At night, the sky was full of searchlights watching for enemy aircraft and zeppelins. This brought the war closer to them. Letters from their loved ones also highlighted the reality of the war as some of the women had relationships with men in army service. Ida Mundell was dating Sergeant First Class Patrick J. Burke of Company A, 319th Engineers, whom she had met some time before the war. Olive Hiatt received letters from First Lieutenant Samuel J. Mustain, of the 135th Aero Squadron, whom she had met on the *Orduna*. Ethel Hiatt was engaged to Private Carl E. Buck of Newcastle, Indiana, who served in the Twenty-Sixth Regiment, First Division, American Expeditionary Forces. Clairette and Simone Hamel had a brother, Private Fernand Hamel, serving in Company D, Nineteenth Battalion, Canadian Expeditionary Forces. Cora's husband, Charles Corson, served in the Seventeenth Infantry Band.

But their lives continued, and they would need to adapt to a new style of theater, audience, and musical tastes. Even the terminology took some time to get used to. Fortunately, American soldiers packed the theaters to see them perform, which helped in transitioning. Unfortunately, they also needed to adapt to frequent German zeppelin and aircraft raids on the city. Everyone around them warned of the dangers from above—and below. For instance, Cora's housekeeper at the Palace Music Hall told them that she would go into the Tube during an air raid. "The people jam in there so thick one can't hardly get their breath. Nearly always someone is killed either trampled on or smothered to death."

Fortunately for the homesick women, London also was the site of a large American YMCA known as Eagle Hut. They frequented this establishment both as a group and individually. The place was packed with American soldiers, so the women did not lack for attention. The men fed the women and took photographs, and in turn the band performed for the boys. While performing there on January 17, Cora met "Mrs. Phillips, a sister-in-law of Waldorf Astor," who invited the women to perform at Westminster Hospital, which was under the direction of the Prince of Wales. On January 22, they obliged and traveled to the hospital to perform for very eager patients. Ida recalled, "They seemed to enjoy it and applauded so loud you wouldn't think they were sick." This would become a trend, and the women would volunteer to travel and entertain the sick and wounded whenever asked.

Their performances in Europe dropped the routines that had started their careers. They did not carry a large caravan for costumes, which limited their acts. They no longer performed Indian songs, dressed in Native garb, or even had a stage of wonderful set pieces. Instead, they focused on technical and popular songs that would showcase their skills as musicians and appeal to patriotic audiences. They did not need to show up the competition with showy performances because theirs was one of the only groups allowed to travel to Europe. Their volunteerism served as their appeal, and they used this to create new popularity in Europe and to reinforce their image back in the United States, where papers and magazines told stories of the brave women who faced submarines and air raids to perform for American and Allied audiences abroad.

On January 28, the women performed at the Metropolitan Theatre as the fourth act in the first show and seventh the second show. Ida Mundell noted that a beautiful skylight above the stage could prove "lovely for an air raid when pieces of shrapnel can come through." After its first performance, the band returned to the dressing room and settled in comfortably. Suddenly, Spahn entered the room and said, "Come on downstairs there is an Air Raid on." They put on their coats and went down to a dressing room on the first floor. Some of the performers sheltered under the concrete stairs. The house manager addressed the audience, telling them not to be frightened, but warned them of the air raid. He told them the show would end due to that lovely skylight, which risked the lives of the artists. The audience of mostly women and children could remain in the building under the balconies until the raid ended.

Just then, the antiaircraft guns began to boom all around the theater. They could hear bombs drop outside with a "big thud." In true Oklahoma fashion, in the spirit of those Oklahomans who go outside at the sound of a tornado siren, the women all wanted "to stick our heads outside to see if we could see some of it but they won't let us." Ida wrote in her journal that women and their children would cry in fright as the guns got louder and the explosions seemed closer, though it seemed to her "funny to be waiting around in a crowd doing nothing."

During the excitement, Glenn Condon walked outside to watch the attack. He told the women that the antiaircraft fire was "all you can see, and they look like a star when they burst. There is so much firing one can imagine they are on the battlefront." Inside the theater, the audience's fear continued to grow. The manager asked if Cora and the band would go out and play, to help ease the tension. They agreed and walked out into the orchestra pit "in our Kimonos, our boots, and our long street coats." The orchestra had disappeared the minute the raid was announced and no one had seen them since. The group played three rags before sitting with the audience and listening to some of the other artists sing.

After their impromptu air raid performance, the theater manager made a speech about how "much pluck the British Artists have to entertain at a time like this and never mentioned we Americans." Unsure whether the manager had forgotten that Cora was American, Condon also made a short speech, informing the audience that they were all Americans and had braved the submarines to get there but that none of them had been the least bit afraid. Once finished, he asked the women to play the American and British national anthems.

At this point, they could still hear the antiaircraft guns firing away but decided to get ready to go home. The firing had stopped by the time they were dressed, and everyone cautiously stepped outside. One of the stagehands stopped Spahn as they left and gave him a piece of shrapnel that had fallen in front of the stage door. They returned to their boardinghouse and were eating dinner when the guns began firing once more. Everyone but the Americans left the house for an air raid shelter across the street. Instead, the band watched out their windows as bombs fell throughout the city. The women had survived their first air raid. Ida recorded the casualties of that night: "98 men, 59 women, and 17 children were injured in the Tubes. 14 men, 17 women, and 16 children were killed in the raid."

Beginning as early as May 15, 1918, papers across the United States reported this as a syndicated story of brave American women who daringly performed through a German air raid. Headlines like "Uncle Sam's Nieces in London Unafraid During Bomb Raid," "Bombs Didn't Scare a Bunch of Pretty Oklahoma Actresses," "U.S. Girls Prevented Panic," and "German Bombs Fail to Scare the Youngblood-Corson Girls" told of their harrowing experience. The women reportedly performed "like veterans" and succeeded "in preserving order."[12] The reported story varied from Ida Mundell's journal entry, however, reflecting the journalistic liberties of the time.

The papers stated that when the air raid warning came, the manager of "a West End theatre" announced that all who like could stay in the theater for shelter, but he would not be responsible for any accidents. The people began to leave, but "the performers in the musical act that had been interrupted" took their instruments and played "the jiggiest, hoppingest ragtime music that they knew." They then "marched into the aisles, still playing." The women then shifted from ragtime to patriotic airs of the Allies, which brought cheers that "drowned out the sound of the gunning and bombing." Other performers on the program came down and sang accompaniment. During this air raid, "Miss Cronk—one of the prettiest of the eight—was missing for a time." She soon returned, carrying a piece of shrapnel she found outside the theater.[13] This version of the story brought immense pride to the families of the women and inspired appreciation of the volunteer efforts of Cora Youngblood Corson and her band overseas.

By February 2, Glenn Condon had received permission to travel to the front lines of France as a guest of the British government. He left with a party of twelve men, half being members of Parliament. On February 6, the women saw firsthand the effects of combat stress upon the men from France. Ida recalled they had seen "a Soldier boy with 'Shell Shock' he was shaking all over could not stand up. An Ambulance come and took him to a Hospital. They say some times the least bit of noise unusual will cause one of those Shell Shock boys to go into a nervous breakdown like that poor fellow was. It is a pitiful sight. He was crying and groaning like he was in terrible agony."

The month of February would prove to be a rough month for Cora and her band as they adapted to their new routine of dodging the frequent air raids. On the night of the February 16, they traveled to the Tube during a raid and stood under a shed to watch the excitement. "We could see the burst in the

Air of the shells. They looked like Stars twinkling . . . It was interesting and rather exciting but was so cold we were about to freeze."

On February 17, the women once again had an exciting night, but this time they had company. The day began at Aldwich Hut, the YMCA for the Australians, where the band performed a short concert to a house full of soldiers. Just as they went outside to leave, the first warning of an air raid was announced. So J. Leslie Spahn went over to the Americans' Eagle Hut and asked if the band could play for them. The octet performed a short concert for the soldiers and a crowd of newly arrived American nurses.

Afterwards, they were sitting down for tea and cakes when the air raid warnings signaled to take cover. The hut had to be evacuated as it was not a safe building during a raid. The women accompanied the soldiers to the Walford Hotel and went down to the Masonic Room in the basement. There, they spent the time entertaining each other by singing or playing piano, and some YMCA men recited. They had such a good time that they "almost forgot there was a raid on." But during their quiet moments, they could hear the guns. By midnight, the all-clear allowed them to start home for a short rest.

The next day, the band performed at the Tottenham Palace Theatre. After their first show, as the women sat down for a snack, the guns suddenly began firing. They realized they had missed the air raid signals. However, the show went on as if the war was not progressing outside. After the group finished its performances, they began their journey home through the Tube, which was filled with people. When the all-clear was given, they had to wait outside the station until the people left the tunnels. Hundreds of people had "been down in there for hours just like rats in a hole." The air "was simply foul and it was almost sickening." Ida remarked that the "poor people are simply scared to death of Air Raids." Without access to a safe shelter, the Tube was the only place to go. The women, however, did not fear the air raids and instead found them "awfully inconvenient and [they] keep us up so late."

Brightening their spirits, Glenn Condon returned from France on the nineteenth, full of war stories and souvenirs. All the women crammed into Spahn's bedroom to hear of his experiences and to look over his relics, including a "a canteen, a helmet, and shells out of an old, demolished tank," as well as some issues of *Stars and Stripes* printed in Paris.

March brought a change of scenery for the women. The group would now begin the Scottish leg of its tour. The first performance in Dundee, Scotland, at the King's Theatre, was a hit with a packed house. Glenn Condon had sailed for the United States on March 12 to travel around Oklahoma and promote patriotism and participation in the war effort. After returning to Oklahoma, Glenn began a speaking tour of the state to raise interest in liberty loans. In Anadarko, the paper announced that he had "been over in France and on the firing line and knows a great deal of what is going on over there."[14] Glenn also brought with him souvenirs of his experience, including a piece of shrapnel gathered after the air raid in London.[15] Glenn's tour added to the reputation of Cora and her group as he spoke of their harrowing adventures.

On April 1, the women experienced a warm welcome from both the locals and American soldiers in Glasgow, Scotland. Cora's name appeared in big electric lights in front of the theater. After the performance, American soldiers lined up outside to speak with the women. Cora reported home that "stage door Johnnies are a thing unknown in England, it seems. That's why it seems so strange to the doorkeepers that we get so many flowers and invitations to dinner. Our Johnnies are the soldier and sailor boys of Uncle Sam. When they see on the program that we're American they want to be clubby right off."[16] This good luck continued as they broke house records by taking encores. In every show, the band would go big. On April 15, a house manager asked the band not to play much ragtime, because of his "refined audience." Spahn convinced him to wait and see how the audience reacted to the music. After the show, the manager said if they changed anything it should be "to put in more ragtime as they seemed to be crazy about it." Their tour of Scotland was a tremendous success.

After they had left Scotland, their train pulled into Liverpool, England. Hundreds of American soldiers lined up on another platform, so the women got out and played "Over There" for them. They then found their next boardinghouse and prepared for another week of performances. On April 30, the group performed at a Canadian hospital for almost one thousand wounded. Some American soldiers also attended the show and brought gifts of sugar, white bread, cake, and candy.

On May 13, Cora and the band learned of their rumored fates. Due to a change of port upon arrival in England, Cora's band had missed its show in Stockport, starting a rumor that they had been killed when their ship was torpedoed. All the acts felt much better after learning of the band's survival. The reputation of these American women had also grown with the British army.

Despite the packed house, several rows would be filled with English officers. Some would write notes to the women, wanting to meet them after the show, but the women would go out the front door to avoid them.

This popularity became so evident that the American vaudeville publications in the United States began to pay attention to the women, despite having excluded Cora during her fight with the VMPA. The *Billboard* reported that Cora and her band were "making a decided hit in and around London, Eng., with their All-American Band." The magazine stated that "they are giving invalided British Tommies a very good sample of what real Western American Girls are like" and that their "offerings are on a par with any male brass band that has gone to that side of the Atlantic to entertain English audiences."[17] The C. G. Conn company also attempted to capitalize by including the band in its publication, *Musical Truth.* The advertisement mentioned that the women had "braved the dangers of submarines and are now playing in the leading theaters of London, England." Of course, the band was completely equipped with the latest Conn instruments, which provided the "inspiring music provided by our American girls" that would "add materially to the patriotic fervor of the Tommies."[18] Cora and her band were actively participating in rallying the English people behind America, and their success seemed, at least to the people in the States, to prove it was working. This renewed reputation proved that the group's gamble to travel overseas had succeeded in helping to repair its reputation after the disastrous last few years with the White Rats.

On May 27, the women traveled to Folkstone, England, which would be the closest they got to the front lines before the armistice. Situated along the coast at the Strait of Dover, the narrowest part of the English Channel, the women could "hear the big guns in France distinctly. They roar like thunder a long way off." At night, they could hear the artillery firing and "could see shells bursting in the sky. They looked like little, tiny stars disappearing quick. We wondered if it was an Air Raid on some French town." Like their time in London dodging air raids, this served as a stark reminder of the fierce fighting happening across the channel.

Many American soldiers trained in this town and readied themselves to embark for France. The women met many talented men, such as Russell E. Levy of the 311th Infantry, a wonderful pianist, and even Jack Keller, shortstop for the New York Giants. They also got into spats with other foreign performers over the integrity of American troops. On June 1, Spahn got into an argument with Laura Novea, a Belgian singer, because after he bragged about American soldiers, she commented that she thought they would not "do any more than the others have." To this, Spahn retorted, "There aren't any spies among them, anyway," and left her. Novea later commented to Cora that he should not brag so much. Cora told her it was none of her business to tell an American citizen what to do.

Perhaps some resentment also existed due to the attention given to the Americans from Oklahoma in English publications. On June 5, Cora graced the cover of the *Performer* once again. June would prove to be quite a month for Americans in the news from Europe. June 6 saw the start of the Battle of Belleau Wood, and newspapers around the world were quickly filled with stories about the United States Army and Marine Corps and their vicious fight to stop the German spring offensive.

On July 17, Cora did something that would appear to be counter to the group's core beliefs, given its work with the White Rats, and performed at a theater while the stagehands were on strike. Before the war, Cora had been a champion of these strikes, but during the war, she seemed to have lost the appetite for such work—or perhaps she did not need to participate because she was already in the spotlight. The manager of the theater had to pull the front curtain himself for the octet's act.

Physically, air raids had drawn the women into the fighting, albeit as passive observers, but the war would soon hit closer to home. On August 5, Ethel Hiatt received the devastating news that her fiancé, Private Carl E. Buck, had been killed in France. He had been wounded during the Battle of Soissons and died of his wounds on July 20, 1918. He was buried in the Aisne-Marne American Cemetery in Belleau, France.[19] Ethel understandably took the news hard and was "all broke up over it. It has only been three weeks since he landed in England. It surely brings this terrible war close to home to us." Despite the somber news, the band determined to go on with its show, continuing the scheduled rounds of performances throughout England and Wales. On October 9, Ida Mundell received word that Joseph Burke was on his way to France.

In England, Cora and her band were not the only female Americans making headlines for their performances. Elsie Janis, the "sweetheart of the AEF [American Expeditionary Forces]," had made a name for herself by traveling to France and entertaining troops on the front lines. She also traveled back to England to perform in musical revues. On October 23, the women all went to see Janis in *Hullo, America*. Janis would become their greatest competition in establishing a reputation for entertaining the troops. However, competition did not worry the women. They were still booked for several months straight. Besides, a new issue started to grow around the world: influenza.

The 1918 flu epidemic hit full swing in late October and would ultimately kill millions of soldiers and civilians alike. Major cities started to take precautions with quarantines, lockdowns, and new laws in the hope of slowing the spread of the disease. In London, "the city soldiers were called out to help take care of the dead, the flu is taking so many that the undertaker can't handle them, and they are running short of caskets." This also meant that people feared gathering in confined spaces, such as the theater.

On November 11, 1918, Cora and her band were on their way to perform at the Stockport Hippodrome outside Manchester, England, when they heard the news that the Germans and Allies had signed an armistice. It did not mark the official end of the war but it meant the hostilities were finally over. As the streets filled with people celebrating the end of the war, Cora and the other women prepared to travel to Ireland. Unfortunately, the women began to show the strain of travel and the flu. They were "tired and sleepy" and were paired with an orchestra whose "leader beats such awful time no one could stay with him." In Dublin, an American soldier came to their show and told them that he had come over on the *Orduna* with them. Since then, he had been to see them perform multiple times. Back in the United States, the *Billboard* reported that Cora Youngblood Corson and her band were "creating a sensation" in Ireland after their performances at the Theatre Royal Hippodrome and Winter Gardens in Dublin. Their performances reportedly "warm[ed] the hearts of the Irishmen and their excellent appearance is being favorably commented upon everywhere they show."[20] This promotion from the *Billboard* indicates that Cora's trip to Europe had worked to get her back into the news and the good graces of vaudeville.

The tour of Ireland ended in mid-December, and the women returned to Manchester. While there, on December 26, they received news that United States President Woodrow Wilson had arrived in London, but they had a matinee performance and could not go see his arrival. However, on December 30, 1918, Wilson traveled to the town hall in Manchester to meet with American citizens who had been invited by the lord mayor. Cora and the women "went around at the front entrance of the Town Hall but could not get very close.

Performing for President Woodrow Wilson. December 1918.
Author's collection.

The crowd was so thick." Spahn quickly thought of an idea and paid a man with a handcart to let them use it as a platform. "It wasn't a very big cart, but it just held we girls . . . Had a fine view above everyone's head." As Wilson arrived, Cora led the band in playing "Over There." "The President smiled and waved his hat at us." As the president continued up the stairs, the band played "The Star-Spangled Banner."

A host of newspapermen and photographers rushed over to speak to and photograph the band. A few cameramen even filmed their impromptu performances. As Wilson left the town hall, they played "Dixie" for him. Leaving the area, the women went to the station and spoke to some Marines from the president's guard. They "had heard about the near-sensation we had created and complimented us on having the nerve to supply the one thing that the local committee had overlooked—music. It was a most wonderful and we shall never forget it."[21] That evening and the next morning, the papers "had some nice write ups and mentioned our little band. Tuesday's *Daily Mail* of Manchester had our pictures in it. The *London Daily Mirror* had our pictures in it and mentioned us as Americans welcoming President Wilson in Manchester."

After this impromptu performance, the group continued with its scheduled tour. On January 6, while performing in Brixton, it encountered a hostile audience that disliked many of the acts on the bill and threw pennies at the performers on stage, including Cora. Ida stated, "They threw pennies at 'Estell Rose' just ahead of our act. So, we got them too . . . They call that 'getting the bird' it is the first time we have ever got it. And it was funny to us." It does not appear that the audience's reaction was a true reflection of the band's performance. Some agents were also present, and after the show they offered Scranton contracts to have the women play "six weeks in South Africa with an option of another month opening there the last of August." The women all signed the contracts the next day.

On April 4, 1918, J. Leslie Spahn secured a five-week contract with the Knights of Columbus, a Catholic fraternal service order founded in 1882. During World War I, the Knights established welfare centers across the United States and abroad for all soldiers, regardless of religion. The organization often provided entertainment at military camps and in major cities. However, the organization only allowed men to join, and the only women associated with the Knights during the war were secretaries—until Spahn secured the contract that made Cora and her band the only female entertainment to perform under the auspices of the Knights of Columbus.

Because of the gender exclusiveness, no female uniforms existed, except for that of the secretaries. Fortunately for Cora, she and many of the women were accomplished milliners and seamstresses. The Knights provided them with permission to acquire various cloth and materials reserved for the war effort to make their own uniforms. On April 26, Cora and Grace went into Manchester for material, where they purchased a light, tan wool used for English officers' pants. They decided to make them "just plain high waisted skirts with two big English Officer coat pockets" with "three quarter length capes with a military collar and the over sea caps." Once they obtained the material, they had only four days to make the uniforms. They did not perform for the next few days, only sewed. They also purchased khaki blouses to go with the suits.

On May 2, the women traveled to the French and British consulates to get their passports approved. On May 3, they worked buttonholes in their uniforms and Spahn purchased some enamel American shields to wear on their overseas caps. They now had the uniforms to go along with their overseas service.

Back in the United States, the success of the Cora Youngblood Corson

Instrumentalists continued to make the news. The *Billboard* reported on the group's contract with the Knights of Columbus:

> Through the efforts of James William Fitzpatrick and Will Conley, the Cora Youngblood Corson Instrumentalists will arrive in France week of May 5, opening in Paris at the big K.C. Theater, which has a seating capacity of more than 3,000. They are to play every camp in France and Germany that has an American soldier in it, and as things now stand it will be the most complete trip ever made by a theatrical company. It will take five weeks, and Miss Corson has offered her services free of charge to the Knights of Columbus.
>
> Miss Corson intended to play for the U.S. boys in July but finding that a great many of them would be going home before that time she made satisfactory arrangements with Mr. Scranton, her agent, and some of the theaters at which she was booked, so that she could make her entertainment tour for the doughboys two months earlier.[22]

On May 4, the women excitedly boarded their transport, headed for France. Their time in Great Britain had garnered them quite a reputation. The *Performer* referred to their act as the "foremost musical act ever sent to Europe from America." The *Tulsa Democrat* went so far as to declare Cora Youngblood Corson "Oklahoma's foremost instrumentalist, who has toured the nation many times with her musical organization composed entirely of women and who gained a nation-wide reputation for her fight against the theatrical trusts."[23] Their successful tour in Great Britain had secured their reputation with the public and showcased their support of American patriotism and volunteerism. Their tour in France and Germany would secure their reputation with the military.

Their crossing of the English Channel and into Le Havre, France, proved to be a smooth journey. Upon disembarking, the women were taken to the head of the queue and had French entrance stamps put in their passports. Shortly after, a Mr. Sullivan, the Knights of Columbus representative who would manage their tour of France and Germany, met them with a Ford truck designed for tours.[24] It had side seats, a top with canvas curtains, and just enough room for the ten women if Sullivan rode up front with the driver.

In Le Havre, they drove to the Knights of Columbus clubhouse that served as their base of operations in the city. There, the women rested and continued "sewing buttons, making buttonholes, and sewing pockets on our uniforms." Their outfits quickly garnered a lot of praise as "the classiest uniforms" in the American Expeditionary Forces. The band gave a short concert at the clubhouse at two p.m. They then spent their afternoon sightseeing in the area. For the first time, they saw French officers "with their light blue coast and bright red pants," and German prisoners. They also visited American graves at the Ste. Marie Cemetery. That evening, they prepared to entertain more troops.

At seven p.m. the group traveled to the Motor Reception House for a concert. The show was originally booked at the Knights of Columbus clubhouse, but the commander, Captain Phillips, said the club was too small to fit all the soldiers. So he gave his troops leave "from 3 P.M until twelve P.M." to "go get their girls and he would have busses and trucks at the Hotel DeVille to carry the crowds out." The result was a packed house with more than two thousand soldiers. The excitement in the air meant that the band played a long concert.

On May 6, the women played a surprise concert for members at the Knights' headquarters in Paris. After lunch, the women met two American officers who were attending the peace conference, so they wandered down to the Hotel de Crillon, where the talks were in progress. Due to their uniforms and their status, American soldiers saluted the women whenever they crossed paths. Cora wrote home that "our K.C. uniforms take us anywhere."[25] On May 7, they traveled to Orly flying field, where Quentin Roosevelt, son of former United States President Theodore Roosevelt, had trained before being killed in an aerial dogfight on July 14, 1918.

On May 8 and 9, they performed at American base hospitals no. 4 and no. 57 as well as at the American military prison. At the prison, they performed in the courtyard so that the prisoners released from confinement "could come to the windows." Afterwards, the women traveled to Cirque de Nouveau, where the Knights of Columbus held prizefights. A packed house of three thousand people greeted the group, which played a concert in the ring before the fight. Then the women watched nine matches. The American boxer Gene Delmont fought against "one of the best" French fighters, de Pontheiu.[26]

On May 11, the women took a trip out to Belleau Wood. This trip to the battlefields of France further ingratiated them with the veterans. They had now served overseas and had seen firsthand the horrors of the war both in England and in France. The women entered Belleau Wood and were immediately confronted with the ghosts of the conflict that had taken place a year prior. "All the way up the hill was holes where machine gun nests had been—one just above the other. Then every so often there would be a trench. On the very top of the Hill is a Tower. It is very battled-scarred [*sic*] but still very pretty good condition. There are four unknown German graves near the tower . . . The trees here are a wreck, so broken and cut to pieces." During their visit, the women all picked up souvenir shrapnel. They also stumbled across a "dead German lying in a trench, he had never been covered and his suit is still looked very good. Mr. Spahn jerked a soldier strap off his suit with his cane." During this trip, Ethel Hiatt visited Carl Buck's grave near Château-Thierry and placed "a lily of the valley and a bead wreath" on his grave.

On their drive back to Paris, they had a bit of excitement as their "truck caught fire from some cause and it was with great speed that we unloaded. The driver had a fire extinguisher on the car, however, and the flames were soon out."[27] Upon their return from Belleau Wood, Sullivan arrived from Le Havre to take charge of their show.

Under Sullivan, the representative from the organization, the group began calling itself the Knights of Columbus Troubadours and prepared to travel to Germany. On May 14, 1919, Ida Mundell recorded that they boarded a train from Paris to Koblenz. After the signing of the armistice on November 11, 1918, the victorious Allies had given Germany thirty-one days to evacuate Belgium, France, Luxembourg, and Alsace-Lorraine and to withdraw their armies from the Rhineland and a neutral zone forty kilometers (about twenty-five miles) from the river.[28] The American Third Army moved toward Germany on November 17, 1918, and took control of the Rhineland alongside a French and British army. The American Army of Occupation was garrisoned at Koblenz and various divisions were billeted in German towns throughout their zone of influence.[29] Cora and her group spent the next two months traveling throughout the region to perform for units of the Third Army.

The Third Army included the First, Second, Third, and Fourth Divisions. However, it would be the Second Division that received most of Cora's time. The last major performer to entertain the Second Division had been Elsie Janis, during the army's stay in the Marbache sector in August 1918. Janis had been brought in by Major General John A. Lejeune, commanding general of the Second Division, to raise morale after the costly battles of Belleau Wood and Soissons. She told jokes, sang, and danced.[30] When they were discussed

Knights of Columbus Troubadours, Le Havre, France. May 6, 1919. Author's collection.

in relation to the "sweetheart of the AEF," Cora and her band were described as "second only to Elsie Janis." Back in Oklahoma, the *Tulsa World* reported that the Cora and her band were "not content with having entertained more American soldiers on foreign soil than any other living woman, with the possible exception of Elsie Janis."[31]

At 12:15 a.m. on May 15, the band's train arrived in Koblenz. The women lined up at the billeting officer's window for their housing, securely placing them "in the army now." Of course, the officer found them a nice, large hotel to stay in for their duration of service in Germany. In Koblenz, the Knights of Columbus had established a comfortable presence by commandeering the local festival hall and even establishing a large doughnut factory capable of turning out more than sixty thousand doughnuts a day. The next day, May 16, the Knights of Columbus Troubadours gave their first concert at the Knights' club. Since it was such a high-profile performance, the "rooms were full. Almost as many doughboys outside as there were in. Also, lots of Germans on the sidewalk." The band's tour in the army started off as a success, and it would continue this trend.

On May 18, the Troubadours performed a matinee in the festival hall, which seated 2,500, packed to standing, making it the largest matinee the American Expeditionary Forces had in that building. It soon became a common theme to play for packed houses. On May 24, in Rhinebrohl, the "little picture house was full, and they were sitting on the floor right up to the stage." On May 26, in Honnigen, "the Theatre was packed. They were sitting on the floor and in the windows and we could see them in the trees outside looking in the windows." To say that the act drew the attention of the men would be an understatement. The group's popularity could not be overstated. Gladys Cronk wrote home, "Lela and I were walking down to eat, our first night here, and in front of us was a boy down on his knees sweeping the dust off the street. He said, 'You mustn't walk on any dirt.' They think a lot of the 'K.C. Girls' as they call us. We are the only K.C. girl entertainers over here."[32]

The group's time in Germany also included many opportunities for personal entertainment. Multiple times during their stay in Koblenz, the women would go on a pleasure cruise up the Rhine river. They also found themselves invited to dances with the men in the Army of Occupation. One night, "the Marines wanted to have a dance and the Artillery men wanted one. So, Mr. Spahn said no to both." Ever persistent, the Marines gathered around their vehicle and "Mr. Spahn finally promised them we could dance a half hour. Went to the YMCA club room . . . Every dance was a tag dance. The hall was about full. Had a great time." Unfortunately, Spahn would not allow the women to attend a ball held by Major General John A. Lejeune, commanding officer of the Second Division, due to the long drive back to Koblenz.[33] Perhaps this was a blessing in disguise, as Ida later wrote, after their first dance with officers, that she would "rather dance with the doughboys. The officers are too much on their dignity." The women also attended a couple of baseball games and boxing matches held by the army and took advantage of being in Germany, visiting many points of interest, such as Beethoven's home.

Being closest to Koblenz, the soldiers, and the Marines and soldiers of the Second Division, enjoyed the music of the troubadours frequently. Traveling to the men sometimes meant travel to castles along the Rhine, like Ehrenbreitstein, where the Seventeenth U.S. Field Artillery occupied the fort. On June 2, 1919, the Second Division held a massive celebration for the anniversary of the Battle of Belleau Wood. In every town that housed troops, entertainment abounded, which included bands but comprised principally

Knights of Columbus Troubadours, Segendorf, Germany. June 2, 1919. Author's collection.

ball games in the afternoon and shows and dances at night. Cora and the troubadours joined in.

After the celebrations, the women continued their scheduled tour of the occupation zone, where the Marines particularly enjoyed the opportunity to entertain the girls. On one such occasion, the women met Captain William B. Croka of the Sixth Machine Gun Battalion, from Hennessey, Oklahoma. Ida Mundell stated that he "was the first Marine Officer from Oklahoma." For their efforts, Cora wrote home that "the Marines want to adopt us, and it is now up to General Lejeune, the commanding officer. It will certainly be nice if they do that, as we will be the only girls thus honored. I will consider it the biggest thing that ever happened to me."[34]

For the next two weeks, the band continued performing in various theaters and camps. However, beginning on June 17, its audience grew exponentially. Traveling to Wehr, the women performed for three thousand soldiers. From June 18 to 20, the octet performed for a combined total of almost 7,500 soldiers at the Andernach Hangar theater.

During their tour in Germany, many of the women in the band began to update their uniforms to reflect their army service. On May 22, 1919, they purchased Third Army insignia patches, which they sewed on the left shoulder of their uniforms, just as the men did to signify the unit they served in. After a while, as Gladys Cronk wrote home, "The boys ask us where our service stripes are—we would be entitled to three now."[35] So some of the women sewed three service stripes onto their left uniform arm to signify more than eighteen months overseas. Finally, a few of the women also wore insignia and medal bars given to them by soldiers or sailors. By the end of their time in Germany, the Cora Youngblood Corson Instrumentalists had essentially earned the accolades of military service through their contribution to the war effort.

After a month of performing across Germany, the group finally returned to France on June 27, 1919. In Paris, the band performed at the Knights of Columbus Circus from July 1 to 4. During this time, they performed for more than 108,500 soldiers. On July 5, they traveled to Brest, to Camp Pontanezen, which served as one of the major debarkation ports for American troops returning to the United States. Here, they opened the Knights of Columbus Carnival, which provided some enjoyment for the tens of thousands of troops waiting for their ship home. A Marine, Private Thomas L. Stewart of the Ninety-Sixth, wrote home of the popularity of the entertainment: "The K.C. has a free carnival every evening out in one of the open lots and it is always crowded."[36] Interspersed with their appearances at the carnival, the band performed for various dances and events, such as at Fort Ferberes Casino, the Thirteenth Marine Battalion dance, the 319th Engineers dance, and General Smedley Butler's hall.

On July 5, 1919, Cora wrote a letter to the *Billboard* to praise the "Stage Women's War Relief," which coordinated the efforts of women volunteers in the theater. The organization had also provided hospital supplies and clothing for soldiers in Europe, conducted liberty loan drives, arranged entertainments and stage performances for troops, and opened a canteen in 1918 for soldiers and sailors in New York City. The gist of her letter revealed that Cora believed that the group had not received enough credit for its role in the war effort. The theater profession had worked tirelessly during the war to raise morale and to support the troops in any way possible.[37] This praise, coming at a time of renewed popularity and overseas service, likely served as a strategic communication to mend Cora's relationship with the *Billboard* after her time in the White Rats.

After a week of performances on land, the band began a "Bon Voyage Tour" to provide entertainment for the men on board the transport ships docked in the harbor. Since the men could not get leave to go to the carnival, the band brought the show to them "through the courtesy and cooperation of the naval authorities."[38] Every day, the "KC Girls" traveled to a new ship and performed on the deck with two other Knights of Columbus entertainers, the Jersey City Police Quartet and Elmer Jerome.[39] Sometimes, such as in the case of the USS *George Washington* on July 25, 1919, Cora and the other women jumped on a small boat and sailed out into the harbor to play for the ship as it left for the United States.[40]

The band closed the carnival on July 26 and entrained to Paris. For the next two weeks, until August 11, 1919, the group performed around Paris for the few remaining American forces. During its time overseas, the band performed "sixty-eight (consecutive) weeks in Great Britain and Ireland, more than 60 concerts for the sick and wounded soldiers. To more than a million Allied Soldiers in France. To more the 75,000 men in the American Army of Occupation in Germany. To more than 10,000 men of the U.S. Navy in the harbors of Europe, Glasgow, Scotland, Queenstown and Belfast, Ireland; Hull, Plymouth, South Hampton and Liverpool, England; Le Havre and Brest, France."[41] This record easily made this band, which began in Anadarko, Oklahoma, one of the most well-known musical organizations in the world. Cora later commented that the military audiences were the most appreciative and "were so nice. So well-mannered. So well-behaved. They never spoke out of turn. They treated the girls in the band like queens."[42]

Before officially wrapping up their tour, "Cora Youngblood Corson's instrumentalists, 10 American girls from the West" gave their final performance at the Knights of Columbus Paris Clubhouse to a large crowd of "gobs" and "doughboys."[43] Finally, on August 12, 1919, after eighteen months overseas, Cora Youngblood Corson and her instrumentalists boarded the *La Touraine*, arriving back in the United States on August 21. This return to the United States countered the contract the band had signed in January 1918 to tour Australia, Italy, South Africa, and Spain after the war.[44] It is not entirely known why Cora seemingly ignored this contract, but the *Chicago Daily Tribune* offered one answer:

> Cora Youngblood Corson sailed on the Touraine today. She is C.D.O. [chief deputy organizer] of the White Rats, the actor's union. She was to sail to South Africa, but letters and cables from the United States have been received and she is going home to help the actors' fight.
>
> She pulled the first strike of actors in Oklahoma City. She is responsible for the Federal Trade Commission investigation. She has been a big factor in the actors' movement in the United States for the last few years.
>
> It is said she came to England to keep the booking trust from getting its hands on papers they were after and to keep the managers' organization, N.V.A. [National Vaudeville Artists], from being taken into the V.A.F. [Variety Artistes' Federation] English Federation. She has little to say about the change in plans for South Africa.[45]

By 1919, in her absence, the White Rats Actors' Union had disbanded due to a lack of funds. The strikes that started in 1916 had failed and the White Rats went bankrupt during the war. The one small success came in May 1918, when the Federal Trade Commission charged that the Vaudeville Managers Protective Association was an illegal operation that restrained trade by forcing performers to pay excessive fees and by placing acts on its blacklist. The result of that hearing forced the VMPA to drop the requirement that a performer must belong to the National Vaudeville Artists to obtain bookings.[46] As a final nail in the coffin, however, Edward Albee acquired the former White Rats clubhouse in 1919 for use as the organization's headquarters.[47] Cora's return came too late to save the White Rats, so she instead turned her attention to returning to the stage in America.

Despite the failures of the White Rats, Cora's success in changing her public image during the war, from a fighting unionist to a volunteer patriot, saved her career. Cora's overseas service in Great Britain and her connection to American troops restored her popularity. By serving overseas, visiting the battlefields, living among the soldiers, and wearing military uniforms bearing service stripes, the Cora Youngblood Corson Instrumentalists had essentially earned the accolades of military service through their contribution to the war effort. By using the war effort to her advantage, Cora had successfully saved her career from following the White Rats Actors' Union into obscurity. She was no longer a troublemaking socialist unionist but a patriotic American veteran of the war.

SIX

THE FALL

hen Cora Youngblood Corson returned to the United States, she needed to find a way to rebuild her career. In postwar America, a new sense of patriotism and nationalism became the norm as Americans began to closely tie themselves to their state. To rebuild her career, Cora reinvented herself by focusing on her wartime service, creating an image as a veteran to draw audiences. With the return of "normalcy" in the country, court cases that had been paused during the war continued. This included a case from the Federal Trade Commission against the Vaudeville Managers Protective Association. However, her efforts in France and Germany in 1919 had left her unable to be a part of the proceedings taking place in Washington, DC, without cutting her engagements in Europe short. In February 1919, therefore, Cora reached out to Oklahoma's Governor Robert Williams for aid in her plight.

In her plea, Cora explained that the band's popularity in Europe offered it the opportunity to travel the world, though she would rather return home. She asked for the governor's support if the VMPA continued to blacklist her upon her return, stating, "I cannot find it in my heart to come home and let that bunch of grafters show the people of the U-S-A that money has beaten me in my fight for right and a square deal."[1] Unfortunately, no response has survived, but Cora did decide to bring her act back to the United States.

The Federal Trade Commission took on the case against the VMPA to investigate "unfair methods of competition in interstate commerce" through its use of fees and blacklists and its monopoly over vaudeville. Despite the evidence and admission of the existence of the blacklist, the commission looked at the case through a single question: Were performances by vaudevillians considered interstate commerce as interpreted in the antitrust laws? Ultimately, the case lasted from February to October 1919 and the commission ruled in favor of the VMPA. With this ruling, all hope for the White Rats Actors' Union faded away and it disbanded as an organization.[2] Cora no longer had a support system to lean on in her fight, which caused her to finally relent and seek employment on the Keith circuit.

Unfortunately, her return coincided with the decline of vaudeville as a form of popular entertainment. The growing popularity of cinema as a cheaper, new form of entertainment meant that more audiences opted to attend a silent film rather than a live performance. Many vaudevillians, lured by more pay and less demanding working conditions, chose to perform their novelty acts for a few moments of screen time. Some vaudeville stars used cinema to launch their film careers, including Judy Garland, Abbott and Costello, and Oklahoma's Will Rogers. Movie stars soon eclipsed the fame of their vaudeville peers.

During the 1920s, most vaudeville shows began to include an equal amount of cinema interspersed with live acts. Historian John Kenrick argues that "top vaudeville stars filmed their acts for one-time pay-offs, inadvertently helping to speed the death of vaudeville. After all, when 'small-time' theaters could offer 'big-time' performers on screen at a nickel a seat, who could ask audiences to pay higher amounts for less impressive live talent?[3] This meant that theater managers began to cut live performances, increasing Cora's difficulty in finding work.

To return to the stage, Cora used her wartime experiences as the new draw for her audience. To audiences and to the local papers, this service equaled active service as a veteran of the war. In Cincinnati, Ohio, for instance, the *Cincinnati Commercial Tribune* announced that each woman was "a veteran of the war!"[4] This fame would transfer well to the states, as Cora could count on the veterans to support her in the theaters.

Oklahoma proudly claimed that its performers had served in the war in various ways and worked to put the state on the map nationally. The *Tulsa Democrat* wrote:

> Although Oklahoma is known in the east generally as a "wild and wooly" country, yet the fact remains that many stars in the theatrical firmament proudly claim this state as their own. Among these might be mentioned Will Rogers, the versatile and original cowboy comedian . . . Elsie Janis is an Oklahoma City girl, although she has not lived there since she was a school child. "Oklahoma Bob" Allbright, one of the best-known singing performers on the Orpheum and Pantages circuits, lives at Nowata, where his mother operates a hotel to this day.
>
> Perhaps the most widely known theatrical woman from Oklahoma is Cora Youngblood Corson . . . who is known as the world's most versatile lady musician . . . She has appeared in public almost continuously now for 13 years . . . In 1917, Miss Corson took her nine girl musicians to Europe. For 16 months she toured England, Scotland, and Ireland, appearing in all the leading theaters of those countries. Every day she played for allied soldiers. Then she went to France for the Knights of Columbus. She has the distinction of being the only performer of her sex to play the "Knights of Columbus Circuit" abroad. She played in Paris and at all the big rest and training camps in France . . .
>
> She is proud of her nativity and always bills herself as "from Oklahoma." Her affections are divided between Tulsa and Anadarko and one city is as much her home as the other.[5]

This positive attention from Cora's overseas tour brought her enough acclaim to return to vaudeville under a new title, the Knights of Columbus Octette. This new octet advertised its overseas service during the war and at home. On September 10, 1919, it had paraded ahead of the Knights of Columbus contingent in New York City for Pershing Day. "The esteem in which Miss Corson and her associates are held was revealed recently when they were asked to lead the K. of C. section in the parade in honor of General Pershing's homecoming."[6] Advertisements noted that they had been "the only woman organization to entertain the A.E.F. [American Expeditionary Forces] in France and Germany under the auspices of the Knights of Columbus."[7]

Cora's return to the stage came as a surprise to some due to her public fight against the VMPA. During her time overseas in 1918, the United Booking Office became the B. F. Keith Vaudeville Exchange, cementing VMPA control over all vaudeville bookings. *Variety* commented on this:

> The Cora Youngblood Corson Sextet opened at Poli's Monday . . . The booking appears to have created some talk among vaudevillians in town . . . The cause of the talk concerning the Cora Youngblood Corson booking that Variety's New Haven correspondent heard, but could not explain, arises through Miss Corson and her act now playing a house (Poli's) booked through the Keith Agency.
>
> An investigation Tuesday made by a *Variety* representative as to the manner in which the Corson turn happened to be booked in a Poli house through the Keith office revealed nothing unusual. P. Alonzo, the Poli booking agent, said the act had been submitted to him and he had been assured the turn would make good. Acting upon this information he had given it two weeks on his time as a trial playing period.
>
> The booking, however, of the Corson act by the Keith Agency, with the booking men understanding that such a contract could not go through unless agreeable to all the powers of the office, seemed to be taken by vaudeville bookers and agents as an indication that though a "blacklist" ever did exist in vaudeville, the last vestige of it disappeared with the placing of the Corson turn in a Keith-booked theatre.[8]

Thus, Cora had finally cut her ties with the White Rats and had succeeded in using her new identification with veterans to remove herself from the blacklist. Just three years prior, in 1917, the VMPA had agreed to pare down its blacklist but had declared that acts described as hardcore White Rats supporters, such as Cora Youngblood Corson, would not be removed from the list.[9] The *Dramatic Mirror* also commented on the new reality for Cora as she played "the 'big time' booked through the B.F. Keith Vaudeville Exchange. This is the same Miss Corson who for a long time was a thorn in the side of the Keith (United) bookers and during the White Rats trouble was an active participant in the 'strike' in Chicago. But the war is over, and the peace dove flies throughout the land."[10]

Furthering the band's association with the war, Cora started her performances with many slides showing the women in various sections of the war zone and the battle-torn countryside, which "brought forth considerable applause."[11] One reviewer for *Variety,* named Bell, wrote a positive review of the act, the first since Cora had started her crusade against the VMPA:

> A slide preceding the act states the K. of C. Octette was the only ladies band to play for the soldiers overseas. Other slides following show the band at Chateau Thierry, Belleau Wood, and other important battle grounds. A drop in one showing the exterior of a Knights of Columbus hut rises, disclosing seven women clad in attractive blue and gold bloomer costumes . . . The act entertained at the Fifth Avenue, closing the show, and should prove a good draw, through its war record, as a feature in the pop houses.[12]

In drawing upon her service overseas, Cora once again reinvented herself as a patriotic world war veteran, which helped her career find its way back on track, just as it had done in the past. By latching onto this new cause and cultural trend of supporting the veterans of the war, Cora successfully convinced potential audiences of the value of her character and performance. This helped audiences, and most importantly theater managers, to move past her former troubles as a member of the White Rats Actors' Union and allow her acts back on the main vaudeville stages.

During this time, Cora also faced the beginning decline of vaudeville. In the wake of theater closures during the influenza epidemic, paired with the ever-growing presence of movies, theaters like the Orpheum circuit suffered a financial crisis. Without the large crowds of the past, theaters could not afford to pay excessive costs for acts. Cora Youngblood Corson, on top of signing to a Keith-owned circuit, also shocked entertainers by drawing a salary out of the Western Vaudeville Managers Association, alongside many other White Rats members who had once stood against the agencies.[13]

This decline also affected Cora's ability to secure long bookings in individual theaters. Her frustration grew until she purchased an entire page in the *Billboard* to advertise her act and its ability. Using the women's overseas experience, she claimed that the 2.5 million soldiers they entertained had not forgotten them and that any time they appeared in a theater "they and their friends and relatives PACKED THE THEATRES." She argued that "at nearly every place we have appeared since our return we have broken all box-office records." She closed with "I say nothing about my act or what it is, but whether it is GOOD OR BAD, I PACK THE THEATRES."[14] This plea signaled the true decline of Cora's career as she attempted to rebuild her tarnished reputation.

In 1920, Cora Youngblood Corson and her Knights of Columbus Octette no longer headlined bills or closed out evenings. But it continued to entertain and play well, with one critic commenting "the act gave a very good account of itself."[15] However, the octet could not bring Cora's career back to its previous height. In May, the women returned to Anadarko to visit family, and it appears they did not leave town for the remainder of the year.[16] Perhaps a long-standing homesickness, partnered with the uninspiring return to the stage, was the cause of this hiatus.

To fill her time, Cora focused on supporting her home state and helping to rebuild an interest in vaudeville. To this end, she began a campaign to establish the Vaudeville Actors' Haven as a retirement community for those in the profession who were no longer able to travel around the country to perform. Cora wanted to make life better for other vaudeville performers who had struggled through the difficulties over the previous few years, including the war and the influenza outbreak. To accomplish this goal, she attempted to create a retirement community in Oklahoma according to a plan she had initially announced in January 1920:

> I have had in mind for the past few years a home for the Vaudeville Actors. One supported by the Vaudeville Actors and the Vaudeville Managers. With this in mind, I have taken up with the Oklahoma representatives at Washington, D.C., the grant of 160 acres of land to place the home on. I have also arranged for plans and the blueprints of same and am now looking forward to its realization.
>
> This Home will not be like any other for the housing of old and sick actors. It will be built on modern plans; its streets will bear the names of "Men" that have been for vaudeville and those that have done things that have and will benefit vaudeville in the future. It will stand as a monument to those that have done and are doing good deeds, and through this movement their deeds will be perpetuated for all time.[17]

Cora hoped that her haven would help bolster not only the state but also the health and job security of those engaged in vaudeville. She favored her home state for many reasons, particularly Oklahoma's geographic location, weather patterns, and reputation, she claimed, as "one of the most healthful States in the union." She also argued that the state provided many opportunities for business that, when taken advantage of, would allow the haven to be self-supporting and even make money.[18] However, given her past issues with vaudeville managers, her campaign to raise funds only targeted the professionals in her field.[19]

To find suitable land for this endeavor, Cora sent letters to multiple Chambers of Commerce around Oklahoma, such as those in Perry and Ponca City, asking for their assistance. Cora estimated that 160 acres and an initial investment of around $100,000 would enable them to build a self-sufficient community with a sizable farm.[20] Cora announced in the *Billboard* that she had received letters of offer from ten towns in Oklahoma and planned to appoint a committee to look them over and "by August 15 decide on the town that is to receive the V.A.H." She outlined her plan for the community:

> The V.A.H. will receive 160 acres free and a five-year option on 320 acres, to be paid for in five years. This will give the Haven Society 60 acres for building and grounds, and 420 acres of farm at the start. There are farms of 160 acres that made $10,000 last year, and will do better than that this year, so I figure that the Haven Society ought to pay for the 320 acres out of its income in the first three years, and the vaudeville actors ought to raise the price of building and stocking the farm at the same time. In that case the Vaudeville Actors' Haven Society would have a piece of property worth at least $300,000 in five years, or three times the invested price in 1925.

Cora believed so much in this idea that she had paid for every cent from her own pocket and was "ready to hand it over to a committee or board that may be appointed to take up where I leave off." She wanted to ensure the separation of actors' and managers' organizations from the haven. Her old grudges against the VMPA showed as she promised the haven would remain "free from domination or dictation on the part of any other combination of actors or managers." This utopian society would "house any vaudeville actor or actress, regardless of their belonging to an organization or not, just so long as the board is convinced that they are vaudevillians and are in need of the care of the Haven." Cora appealed to her fellow vaudevillians to show the world that they were willing to do "something for your brother and sister artists of today and in the future."[21]

Despite this plea, the Haven gained no real traction with the vaudeville community. Cora attempted to save it one last time by writing a letter that was published in the *Billboard:*

> I wish those that oppose the founding of the V.A.H. would come out in the open and state what objections they have to the same, or if they have anything to offer that would be an improvement or would in any way help the promotion of the same would give their ideas on same, and I would only be too willing to hand over my part in it, just so long as it would remain out of the hands of any other organization or combination of men that would show favors to anyone.[22]

Unfortunately, it seems that Cora's dream did not pick up enough support and it died away after August.

The latter half of 1920 found Cora floundering for some sort of identity or goal as she came to terms with the loss of her high-profile vaudeville career. Strangely, it seems she decided to part ways from her band and from her work on the Vaudeville Actors' Haven. In October, the *Oklahoma City Times* reported that she had traveled to Providence, Rhode Island, where she played baritone cornet in a ladies' band, "winning much fame."[23]

In November, she again wrote to several Chambers of Commerce in Oklahoma, but this time for the purpose of finding "six towns in Oklahoma to promote a girl's band of 25 or more girls in each town." She wanted to organize this large band to compete in an organization called the National Organization of Woman's Amateur Musical Organizations, which would "hold conventions each year" and give "prizes to the best bands and orchestras." She wanted Oklahoma to be represented. She planned to take the top talent from the six towns for competitions and "at the same time have the largest organization in America by combining the six." Ultimately, Cora wanted to "put Oklahoma on the map as a musical state."[24] However, it does not appear that anything came of this attempt and Cora returned to Anadarko by December, where she performed for local meetings like the young men's class of the M. E. Sunday School pie supper.[25]

By 1921, Cora had picked up with her band once more but dropped the Knights of Columbus Octette name and performed as the Cora Youngblood Corson Orchestra. However, the group continued to push its popularity with military veterans. Now back in Oklahoma, the band played at various American Legion halls. To advertise the show, the papers called back to the band's time overseas, with comments such as "of American Expeditionary Forces fame" and "the same organization which played for the Army of Occupation in Germany."[26] It appears that the band was struggling to find gigs under Cora's leadership and so staged small, local performances. For instance, in March, the group performed "dances every Saturday night, from 9 to 12, in the Dining Room of the Bryan Hotel."[27] This was vastly different from Broadway.

Another life adjustment came on March 15, 1921, when Cora divorced Charles Corson. Their lives had taken them into constant routines of travel since their marriage. As they toured different portions of the country, they saw less and less of each other. While she continued to send him postcards and letters, they did not see enough of each other. In a letter to Charles, she wrote:

> Do not be too terribly surprised upon receiving this letter and contents: If you will sign this waiver and return it to me, you will be a free man about May. I think 17 years of unmarried-married life is quite long enough don't you. I hope you will be more fortunate in the future and always think of me kindly. I tried but failed.[28]

With this, Cora closed a chapter of her life, but she continued to carry the Corson name.

Strangely, in May 1921, the group returned to playing in theaters, but in a show presented by E. Gracia Acton, who had been a trombonist in the band. On May 8, the Empress Theater in Springfield, Missouri, advertised "E. Gracia Acton presents The Girls from the Golden West in Frolics on the Roof in New York." The show was a twenty-person "musical comedy company" that headlined Ernie Devoy and Harry Reader and featured Cora Youngblood, "prima donna and musical artiste supreme."[29] It is an odd moment in which Cora is no longer in charge of her own group and is not the headliner.

On November 11, 1921, Cora once again reinforced her association with the war as part of the ceremonies in New York that aligned with the opening of the Tomb of the Unknown Soldier in Arlington National Cemetery in

Washington, DC. In Times Square, the center of New York's theater district, Cora joined several speakers to remember the sacrifices made by soldiers and noncombatants. She represented the Knights of Columbus and the women who served overseas.[30]

After this event, Cora remained in New York and participated in the creation of the Oklahoma Society of New York, alongside ex-Governor Charles Haskell and other influential Oklahoma expatriates.[31] In the 1920s, Oklahomans sought to reinforce their ties to Oklahoma regardless of their location. Enthusiastic patriotism brought pride in their native state and offered many people a cultural identity beyond their current locale. The Oklahomans looked to reinforce their connection to their home state and its values of rugged entrepreneurship, which was encompassed by the state motto "Labor omnia vincit" or "Work conquers all."

This group was formed to "preserve the history and traditions of the state of Oklahoma," since so many performers and celebrities had moved out of the state.[32] To accomplish this, the group worked to "aid in compilation and preservation of data, reminisces, photographs, and documents of historical value in the hands of New Yorkers who were among Oklahoma's '89ers' and to aid Oklahoma people whenever they come here to visit or to live."[33] The group opened its doors to all former and current residents of Oklahoma and anyone interested in learning more about the state.

Cora's brother-in-law, Glenn Condon, took up office in the organization as chairman of the press. Finding an opportunity to once more reinvent herself as a Native American and create interest in her performances, Cora reasserted her false connection to a Native heritage and its coexistence with being an Oklahoman. During the final meeting of the organization, Cora and her sister Eula performed alongside Chief Michael Martin Silvermoon, an artist of the Caddo tribe, also from Anadarko. They performed "an original Indian folk song, in the native tongue." This is the first time Cora was presented in a Native language alongside a Native performer. During the meeting, Condon also delivered an address on the "importance of Oklahoma to the theatrical profession." Among those mentioned were Bob Albright, Cora Youngblood Corson, Buster Keaton, Pawnee Bill, and Will Rogers.[34]

More than two hundred former Oklahomans joined the organization and attended their entertaining gatherings. Many high-profile individuals from Oklahoma came to speak at these meetings, including Senator James W. Ge-

Cora Youngblood Corson (*center*) with Miss Chickadee and Mrs. Red Eagle. *Pittsburgh Press.* January 29, 1922.

rard, ex-Governor Charles Haskell, Congressman Joe C. Pringey, and others.[35] On January 17, 1921, the society held a "Cherokee Dance" at the Hotel McAlpin in New York City.[36] The main feature of this midwinter festival "was Native Indian dances by fully garbed Indian men and women of various tribes. Native Indian songs were enjoyed by the huge attendance of former Oklahomans and others interested in the traditions of the state."[37] Reportedly, more than a dozen "Oklahoma Indians" performed for the society.[38] Cora was among these performers. An image of her in full Native dress shows two other women similarly dressed, with the caption "Cora Youngblood, Cherokee; Miss Chickadee, Sioux; and Mrs. Red Eagle, Indian women in a N.Y. Park."[39] This was the first time Cora had presented herself as a member of a particular tribe, likely emboldened by the society's acceptance of her act and by the necessity to revive her own fame.

Cora's performance as an "Oklahoma Indian" marked the acceptance of her Native representation not only by those in New York, who likely knew nothing of actual Native culture, but also by her peers from Oklahoma. She had once been either Native American or an Oklahoman, but now she fell solidly into the "both/and" category. To the audience, she was both a performer and a Native. If Cora claimed a heritage and displayed some intimate understanding of that heritage, then it seems not to have been questioned by the audience or by her peers. Her performance with Native musicians and dancers seems to show that perhaps they too were fooled by Cora's persona, or perhaps they simply played along for the act. If she could establish some anchor within her newly chosen community, then it appears people believed she had the authority to make her claims of belonging.

Three months later, the society celebrated the "opening of Oklahoma to the white man" with an Eighty-Niner dance, displaying the sense of a dual identity for Oklahoma. To "properly" celebrate the event, the dance began with men and women splitting to the sides of the room and then running to the middle to "lay claim to a dancing partner."[40] The dance also featured more Native performers, including Princess Atalie Unkalunt, a Cherokee opera singer from Stilwell, Oklahoma. At around ten o'clock, the band stuck up an Indian song, and in through the door "marched a troupe of full bloods, attired in tribal costumes." Chief Sheet Lightning (Walter Battice), a "well-known Sac and Fox performer and activist" and the purported leader of this troupe, spoke on the days of the past never to return and of the love the Indian had for the state of Oklahoma.[41] Next, Weather String, a World War I veteran, delivered a speech on "the Indian's affection for his white brethren." The Indians then performed a "war dance" before leaving the room, after which, poetically, in rushed a group of cowboys, firing their pistols in the air.[42]

Despite these performances in New York, Cora and her group continued to find difficulty in vaudeville and experienced many falls from their pedestal, such as the loss of headlining engagements. On top of this, Cora's manager, J. Leslie Spahn, began to have public financial troubles. In December 1921, Spahn was sued by Adele Sturtivant for $950, "alleging back salary and breach of contract. The plaintiff claims she was booked by Mr. Spahn February 26 for twenty weeks, from April 2, with the act, 'The Girls from the Golden West,' at a salary of $50 a week, and that on April 30 she was discharged without cause."[43] On February 18, 1922, the *Billboard* also announced that "J. Leslie Spahn . . . this week filed a petition in bankruptcy."[44]

Despite her manager's problems, by the fall of 1922 Cora had returned to a sextet. With the struggles in vaudeville, Cora looked for other opportunities for the band to perform. She still maintained her farm, which provided secure financial backing during this period, so she could explore any avenue to return to fame. She found opportunities with the Shriner's Circus, with which the band signed a two-year contract.[45] The group traveled across the country with the circus, performing in smaller venues like a Kiwanis Club meeting in Sioux Falls, South Dakota.[46]

The *Tulsa World* praised Cora's performance at the circus and wrote of her past success: "The leader of this popular aggregation is a native Oklahoman, who has won fame and fortune in the musical world and who is known from coast to coast."[47] In December 1922, however, Spahn announced to the *Billboard* that Cora would be leaving the Shrine Circus to perform for Moore's Indoor Circus.[48] During this time, Cora continued to find new opportunities to perform in Oregon and Washington, such as on radio. Like the rising popularity of film, radio also contributed to the decline of audiences at vaudeville acts. Music could now be broadcast directly into people's houses, so they no longer needed to dress up and go to a crowded venue. In Oregon, the band performed for KGG Radio a piece arranged by W. A. McDougall of the McDougall–Conn Music Company.[49]

In August 1923, Cora and her group returned to their tried-and-true format of performing at fairs, beginning with the Andrew County Fair in Missouri in the later part of the month. After finishing their gig in Missouri, they moved to perform at the Nebraska State Fair every afternoon and evening.[50] Interestingly, it appears that Cora once again projected a Native American heritage in her act, performing at the Andrew County Fair alongside a woman named Princess White Cloud, described as a "an Indian contralto," who sang popular songs and was purported to be from the Sioux tribe.[51] This adjustment may have come from Cora's return to the Midwest, where a Native persona could draw more crowds.

It certainly seems to have worked, as performing alongside Princess White Cloud seems to have brought out the old tropes of Cora and her heritage. The *Lincoln Journal Star* announced that "Miss Corson is a full blooded Cherokee Indian."[52] These performances with Princess White Cloud offered Cora an opportunity to revamp her stale act by once again promoting Native American headliners, as she had done early in her career. Cora and her group performed after Princess White Cloud and made quite the impression on guests. Cora played her double euphonium and the saxophone with the sextet, but her signature tuba act stole the show. "Miss Corson was dressed in white and made a striking picture with the gold coils of the instrument wrapped about her body snake fashion as she plays."[53]

From Nebraska, the Cora Youngblood Corson Sextette traveled to Indiana to start a new tour. While on their way to Indiana, Cora and the band stopped at the Drake Hotel in Chicago to visit Midwest Radio Central, which broadcast their act across the Midwest.[54] Unfortunately, despite their attempts to embrace this new medium for their act, Cora and her acts did not achieve radio fame.

In 1924, Cora continued to adapt the group with an eye toward staying popular. In January, they performed as Cora Youngblood Corson and Her Oklahoma Belles, headlining at the Family Theater in Rochester, New York.[55] In April, the group briefly dropped its unique group act and joined a production called *Giggles,* described as a burlesque attraction.[56] Early in Cora's career, the idea of a burlesque show kept her from looking toward vaudeville as a career. However, with the rapid decline of vaudeville's popularity, it seems Cora began to look anywhere she could for a performance opportunity. Presented by Joseph Levitt Attractions, *Giggles* promised to be a show of "beautiful girls, exquisitely gowned, fascinating music, wonderful dancing," and sure to be "frisky, brisky burlesque."[57] Critics praised the comedy and music of the act and claimed that though it was not top-notch, it easily qualified as "a good average burlesque show."[58]

After a short couple of weeks performing in the show, Cora and her group continued on their own tour through April and May.[59] In June, Cora signed her group to be a part of Frederick V. Bowers's *Kiss Me Again Revue,* an "unusual vaudo-musical-song show" that included many different performers.[60] The group toured across the Midwest until July.[61] While touring with this production, Cora and her group were presented as Cora Youngblood Corson and Her Petticoat Band.[62] Another advertisement called them Cora Corson Youngblood and Her Girls' Jazz Band. Cora had adopted popular jazz melodies into their repertoire, along with their traditional brass and opera selections. The players also took the show into the crowd by performing while walking through the seats to open the production.[63]

As 1924 came to a close, the group continued to perform on its own in the Midwest and Northeast.[64] It also picked up gigs at some fairs. While the band was engaged at the Lake County Fair in Indiana, the newspaper commented on Cora's fall from grace due to her union activism, and in an article sure to have stung Cora's pride, it placed her new situation in its context: "The Cora Youngblood Sextette of girl musicians are the headliners of the vaudeville

Cora Youngblood Corson and Company. 1924.
C. G. Conn advertisement. Author's collection.

show. For years Cora Youngblood was in big time vaudeville but since her activities in organizing the performers she has played the fairs."[65] This unfortunate article shows the extent of Cora's fall because of her attempts to better the lives of vaudeville actors. Ironically, shortly after this performance, the band booked a tour on the Keith circuit, which was owned by one of the men who opposed the White Rats so thoroughly.[66]

In November and December, the band went to New York to participate in a promotional campaign for C. G. Conn's fiftieth anniversary. The women posed for promotional photographs while holding their various instruments. One of these images was made into a postcard advertisement that read "A trip around the World with Conn Instruments. Manufactured at Elkhart, Indiana. Cora Youngblood Corson & Co."[67] In addition to the photographic advertisements, Conn created a large sousaphone to celebrate its anniversary. This commemorative instrument was gold plated with silver highlights and engraved by Conn's master engraver, Julius Sternberg, to depict scenes from the company's history. It was claimed that this was "the largest and most beautiful tuba ever built," even rivaling Cora's sousaphone.[68] Because of her skill, Cora was invited to play the tuba in New York.

The public attention likely translated well into her performances in 1925. In January, the group headlined a vaudeville show in Yonkers, New York. The papers declared that the group was "a headliner of considerable prominence and merits a place among the most sought-after of all vaudeville productions."[69] For the next three months, the group toured through New York, Pennsylvania, Connecticut, and surrounding states with great success. At this point in its career, the band became popular for being "versatile musicians who play everything from opera to jazz."[70] The papers began to be much kinder than they had in years prior. In New Jersey, the *Morning Call* announced that Cora "is one of America's foremost musical conductors. In fact, she was one of the first and undoubtedly one of the most successful women in this artistic calling."[71]

Just a few months later, on February 8, Cora's mother, Sarah Jane Youngblood, died.[72] Then, in June, the health of Cora's father, Jeremiah Youngblood, took a turn for the worse and she canceled her tours to return home. On July 8, he died due to heart failure, with Cora at his bedside.[73] Owing to this unscheduled return to Oklahoma, when the band began touring once more, they started locally before moving through the Midwest.

They began in Kansas before returning to headline at the Orpheum Theater in Oklahoma City.[74] While in Oklahoma, Cora was interviewed by the *Oklahoma News*, which pointed out the various instruments she now played in the band: "Mrs. Corson plays the tuba, cornet, saxophone, euphonium, bagpipes, and cello."[75] In 1926, the band continued its tour, and the papers in the Midwest once again began to describe Cora as a Native American. In St. Joseph, Michigan, she was described as "of the Cherokee race."[76] In Benton Harbor, Michigan, she was "a full blood Cherokee Indian."[77] Cora could draw in crowds that expected to see the stereotyped image of a Native and an Oklahoman on stage. In February, the group ended its tour of the Midwest and moved south to Kentucky as a headliner on the Keith circuit.[78]

By 1927, however, Cora's band was taking its last gasps. Playing as the headliner was no longer the norm. While in New York, the band received what may have been the last article dedicated to its performance. The Johnstown *Morning Herald* announced that the bill booked at Smalley's theater would be "the best all-around vaudeville entertainment that has so far been presented this season." Cora Youngblood Corson and Her Sextette headlined the bill. The paper announced that she would be playing the large sousaphone during their performance and ended by stating, "This act is America's leading Lady Band."

Interestingly, in line with the rise of movies in vaudeville theaters, in the same advertisement, Smalley's announced its showing of *Corporal Kate.* This film about the "women's side of the World War" details the story of two women who go to the front as entertainers. The story of the film mirrors Cora's: The women decide to support the troops by performing overseas. While there, they have difficulty finding accommodation. Their performances are generally appreciated by the soldiers but sometimes the crowd goes against the group. Finally, the women are subjected a German air raid, during which one is killed. Fortunately for Cora, no one had been killed during her time in Europe.[79]

On May 10, 1927, it appears that Cora and her band performed together for the last time as a group. Cora Youngblood Corson's Band performed as the Syncopated Bully Girls in Herbert Hall Winslow's comedy *He Loved the Ladies.* This play at the Frolic Theatre in New York fared poorly in reviews, with critic Rowland Field stating of the performers, "There are one or two others in the cast who have their moments in the play, but the assemblage, taken as a whole, is not so good. In fact, there are those who are terrible, if you must have the truth."[80] As for Cora and the women's performance, J. Brooks Atkinson, another critic, wrote, "The Syncopated Bully Girls in harlequinade costume, whom one had been anticipating, are so far backstage that one cannot see them clearly."[81]

With this final review of their performance together, it appears that the group that had toured and performed continuously for twenty years, albeit with a varying cast of women, finally decided to retire the act. It is unclear when exactly the band stopped performing together, as one article on September 19, 1928, mentioned the women of the "Cora Youngblood-Corson Concert Band" returning to visit Anadarko.[82] However, I have been unable to find any more advertisements for the group in newspapers after 1927. This aligns with the purchase of the Keith-Albee-Orpheum Theatres Corporation and its consolidation into Radio-Keith-Orpheum (better known as RKO) by Joseph P. Kennedy Sr. from 1926 to 1928. This hostile buyout brought under Kennedy's control more than seven hundred theaters, which he converted to cinemas.[83] After entertaining audiences around the world—millions of people—this successful and outspoken band faded from public memory.

SEVEN

RETIREMENT

By 1927, Cora's career in vaudeville had ended, and with it her entire persona as a vaudeville performer. By this time, Cora and her family had moved to Tulsa, leaving behind their farms and any social ties to the tribes of Anadarko. Despite Cora's professional downfall and misfortune, the state of Oklahoma boomed with the discovery of the world's largest oil reserves in Seminole County in 1926 and 1927, and the state returned to the national stage as one of the biggest oil producers in the world. As Oklahoma prospered, so too did the nation, and unbridled economic prosperity continued to rise. Cora attempted to find her place in this new era without vaudeville but struggled to establish herself. Likewise, many Native tribes continued to look for a participating role in an ever-changing national identity.

The American public's obsession with Native Americans in the early twentieth century came from the myth of the "vanishing Indian," a self-fulfilling prophecy that paralleled "manifest destiny." As territorial expansion by white settlers and violent conflict pushed Native Americans further west, an influential cultural myth took root that Indigenous peoples would likely disappear through conflict, disease, or assimilation. For example, in 1925 Famous Players–Lasky produced the film *The Vanishing American,* based on Zane

Grey's book of the same name, which highlighted the American government's negative portrayal of Native Americans. In the 1920s, the consumption of Native American material reached a new height as popular culture evolved.

The obsession of white Americans "to consume performances of racial and ethnic differences rendered in musical terms" provided a perfect opportunity for Native musicians.[1] Music became a way to sell "expectations about Indianness," and Native people "were involved in recording, contesting, affirming, transforming, controlling, and performing those expectations in critical ways."[2] "All-Indian" bands began to spring up to perform popular music genres around the country, and eventually internationally.

Taking advantage of this opportunity, Joe Bayhylle Shunatona, a Pawnee Otoe bandleader, formed the United States Indian Reservation Band, also sometimes referred to as an orchestra, in the late 1920s. Shunatona received his musical education as a student at the Chilocco Indian Agricultural School in northeastern Oklahoma. He excelled on several instruments and left Oklahoma to attend a music conservatory in Wichita, Kansas. In 1918, he graduated in elocution and dramatic arts and moved to New York state to study grand opera with baritone Oscar Seagle. Upon entering the musical scene, however, he could not find footing in "serious" art music and instead moved toward the "show Indian" trajectory, performing in the Oklahoma-based 101 Ranch Wild West Show. He followed this with a stint on the vaudeville stage until moving to New York City in the late 1920s. In 1929, Shunatona secured a tremendous gig: to take an "all-Indian" band to perform at the inauguration of President Herbert Hoover and Vice President Charles Curtis.

In the 1928 presidential election, Republican Herbert Hoover had defeated the Democratic nominee, New York Governor Al Smith, in a landslide election, making major inroads in the South. For his Vice President, Hoover chose Charles Curtis, who became the first Native American to be elected to that office. The selection of Curtis, as a Native American, may have aided in the popularity of the nominees in Oklahoma, where Hoover carried sixty-six counties out of seventy-seven, with only the southeast portion of the state voting for Smith. It proved to be the first election since its statehood in which Oklahoma had voted more Republican than the national average.[3]

Charles Curtis was born on January 25, 1860, in North Topeka, Kansas Territory, as a member of the Kaw Nation. His mother, Ellen Pappan, had Kaw, Osage, Potawatomi, and French heritage. When Curtis was three years old, his mother passed away, after which he went to live with his grandparents on the Kaw reservation while his father, Orren Curtis, fought in the Civil War. On June 1, 1868, Charles Curtis witnessed a large band of Cheyenne warriors invading the Kaw reservation. During the skirmish, Curtis accompanied Joe Jim, a Kaw interpreter, as they sought assistance from the Kansas governor. He later likely witnessed several more battles and deaths in tribal conflict involving the Cheyenne.[4] Due to the violence, Charles was sent to live with his other grandparents in Topeka, where he obtained an education in the local schools. During his teens, Curtis rejoined the Kaw nation, which had been removed into Indian Territory.

As a result of his own life experience, Curtis believed in assimilation policies and pushed for the education of Native children. In 1892, as a member of the United States House of Representatives, Curtis sponsored the Curtis Act of 1898. Curtis's election to vice president brought a new spotlight to Native culture and its acceptance by the federal government. The invitation of the United States Indian Reservation Band to the inauguration provided the opportunity for its members to represent and celebrate the country's Native duality. As John Troutman argues in *Indian Blues: American Indians and the Politics of Music, 1879–1934*, "The practice of music, in a very real sense, provided a means by which American Indian people could strategically deploy their newfound U.S. citizenship—for example, to reinforce their tribal identities—in the face of OIA [Office of Indian Affairs] officials who sought to dismantle that core of their existence."[5]

To form his "All-Indian" band, Shunatona searched around Oklahoma and created a group of twenty musicians, most from the northeastern part of the state. Financed by William G. Skelly and an associative group of representative Tulsans, Shunatona's Indian Reservation Band started for Washington, DC, in February 1929.[6] Newspapers heralded this organization as "twenty real, genuine, 100 percent Americans, the kind that wear feather head-dress, beaded head-bands, buckskin-woolen garments, gaudy blankets, and moccasins in their western habitat . . . This visiting all-American delegation, a veritable league of tribal musicians representing 16 states and 15 Indian tribes of the western states, is the sensational United States Indian Reservation Band, which only seven months ago was scattered all over the wild and wooly west."[7] Audiences would be in for a treat to see a representative organization of Oklahoma's tribal nations serve as delegates on a national stage.

The United States Indian Reservation Band (Cora with tuba). Around 1928. Courtesy of the Museum of Tulsa History.

Originally, it was intended that the only woman in the band, Princess Red Eagle, who sang "both contralto and baritone," would attend the inauguration.[8] However, for some unknown reason, Cora Youngblood Corson replaced her. As a member of this organization, Cora assumed a new persona to be more Native. On their way to Washington, DC, the band performed at several vaudeville theaters. While in South Bend, Indiana, the paper printed a photograph of the band with the names and tribes of its members. Sitting in the middle of the front row is Cora Youngblood Corson, but the article calls her "Wildflower, a Cherokee, who punishes one of the largest tubas ever made for any man and incidentally is a baritone and euphonium soloist."[9] The image and description are undoubtedly Cora.

Not only had she chosen a new name but she now belonged to a specific tribe. This reflects Cora's loss of self with the decline of vaudeville. Previously, she had not publicly claimed to be a member of any tribe. During her career, articles had proposed many different tribes but she did not seem to confirm or deny their assumptions. During her early career, Cherokee would not have been the most obvious choice, since that tribe occupied northeastern Oklahoma whereas Cora lived in Anadarko among the Apache, Comanche, and Kiowa. But since she had moved to Tulsa, Oklahoma, in the heart of Cherokee country, she had an opportunity to create a new perception of herself that might afford her a new avenue back into vaudeville. The opportunity to join a local Indian band for national tours meant that Cora needed to "become" Native if she wanted to get back on stage. Simple ethnic impersonation, just being "Indian," would not be effective in this new environment. Therefore, by firmly assuming Cherokee heritage, Cora could take advantage of the growing popularity of Native performers to return to vaudeville after her career had faded away.

To illustrate this point, Cora chose the name Wildflower as her new Cherokee persona. It evokes the image of the stereotyped "Indian songs" of her early career. In fact, in 1908, E. Ray Goetz and Lou A. Hirsch released the Indian song "Wildflower," featuring the stereotypical Indian maid with a headband and feathers on the cover, which Cora emulated during her time with the Indian Reservation Band.[10] However, the name Wildflower did not last long and the papers began calling her Princess Youngblood. Cora even had professional photographs shot in New York in her regalia, and these are labeled "Princess Youngblood." Cora fully embraced this Indian image and chose a title that reflected the stereotypical idea of Native performers. This propelled her back into the spotlight.

Despite the name change, Cora's reputation as a musician preceded her, and the papers continually commented on her skill. She was known as the "Oompah Squaw" or the "Oompah Princess" in reference to the rhythmic sound of a tuba, popular in German music.[11] Carrying her large sousaphone, Cora marched with the band in the inaugural parade while blimps and airplanes filmed the procession on March 4, 1929.[12] Alongside their appearance in the parade, the "Indian Reserve Orchestra" performed together with other band at the Rialto Theatre on March 3 and 4. This multiband performance provided the inaugural visitors an opportunity for "patriotic pride and lofty idealism."[13] But the existence of the Indian band also celebrated "the Native identities that the same government had spent the last fifty years seeking to destroy."[14] As William K. Powers argues, "For all Natives, music *is* culture, and all musicians are the culture's custodians."[15] Cora and the Indian Reservation Band became the representatives of Native culture on a national stage.

Princess Youngblood. Around 1928.
Author's collection.

After the inauguration, Cora continued to tour with the band on the Radio-Keith-Orpheum circuit.[16] During this tour, the band also performed for radio stations such as WCAE in Indiana, Pennsylvania.[17] While set to perform at the Prospect Theatre in Brooklyn, New York, the local paper commented on the presence of the Indian band at the inauguration stating, "If visitors at the recent inaugural ceremonies in Washington were curious about recurrent sights of feather head-dress, gaudy blankets, and war paint on bronzed faces, they should have known that beneath these blankets and feathers could be found American clothes of the most modern design. The 'scary injuns' were, in reality, but the members of the United States Indian Reservation Band."[18] Native Americans continued to struggle to overcome the stereotypes of "savagery" that still plagued public perception.

The group's musical act, *From Camp to Campus,* received positive reviews from critics, with Chief Roaring Thunder and Princess Youngblood heralded as the talented entertainment assisting the band.[19] As the group traveled along the circuit, it performed at many theaters that Cora had headlined almost two decades prior. Cora's name was back in the headliner position for theater advertisements, but this time as Princess Youngblood.[20] The band performed jazz, solos, and vocals. Will Abel, a critic for *Variety,* commented that the band "sure know their jazzique." He also spoke favorably of Cora's performance, stating that Princess Youngblood, "who does 'Old Black Joe' as a Sousaphone solo is announced as being the only woman to master this instrument, in addition to playing the largest of its kind. She clicked."[21] The papers also reflected these reviews of Cora as they commented that she "plays skillfully on a great instrument few women could handle."[22]

On April 9, 1929, the United States Indian Reservation Band arrived in Boston, Massachusetts, for a performance at the local theater. While there, the band met with local government officials, placing themselves as representatives beyond the stage. First, they met Massachusetts Governor Frank G. Allen, who presented Cora with "a gold pin bearing the seal of the Commonwealth." They then went to city hall, where they met with Mayor Malcolm E. Nichols.[23] The next day, April 10, the band traveled to Northampton, Massachusetts, where it serenaded former President Calvin Coolidge during a snowstorm. After playing one song, Coolidge shook hands with "Chief Shunatona, leader of the band, and Princess Young Blood, a Cherokee."[24] Once finished, the band continued onward for more theater performances.

The popularity of the band continued to grow after the performance for Coolidge, and Cora once more became the topic of discussion whenever the band found mention. In Brooklyn, one critic for *Variety* commented that the band "gave plenty of color to the finish" of the bill. In his opinion they were, rightfully, taking advantage of the "bushels of page one publicity" they had received. He also noted that "Princess Youngblood, who plays the giant Sousaphone and is the single feminine member, bears great resemblance to Cora Youngblood Corson."[25]

This remark demonstrates an interesting issue in pinpointing Cora's perceived heritage. Obviously, the reporters knew that Princess Youngblood was Cora Youngblood Corson. However, there is no questioning of this name change. Perhaps the reporters knew that it was just an act, or maybe, like many of her audiences early in her career, the public had accepted that Cora was a Native American from Oklahoma and therefore that her participation in this organization was a natural fit. Supporting this idea is the repeated assertion in the media that the group was made of "100% Natives."[26] There was no reason to question the name change of a woman who many already believed had Native ancestry.

As the band continued to tour, the papers announced the band's scheduled April 28 performance at the Palace Theater in Chicago. The article noted that "featured with the band is Princess Youngblood (Cora Youngblood Corson)." It also noted that "Miss Corson for several years had her own band."[27] Her false Native heritage did not come into question in this professional publication either, though when the band ventured elsewhere in the Midwest, more disparaging rhetoric regarding Natives replaced the praise of the act in the papers, especially with regard to Cora. On August 11, 1929, the *Cincinnati Enquirer* commented, "Even in their theatrical endeavors the Indians cannot get away from the idea that the squaw should be allotted the heavy duty. The heaviest feature in their routine as the Indian Band, permits the redskins to shoulder onto Princess Young Blood, their feminine star, what is said to be one of the world's largest tuba horns."[28] The paper also commented that the band would perform "jazz played by real savages" and that Cora was "an 'original' American prima donna."[29] This act in Ohio appears to be the final performance of Cora with the United States Indian Reservation Band in 1929, as she does not appear in anymore advertisements moving forward.

After her departure from the band, Cora reformed her own group, the

Cora Youngblood Corson Band, composed of ten women. Beginning on August 22, 1929, advertisements announced that Cora's "world famous band" would be performing at the Cuming County Fair in West Point, Nebraska, from August 26 to 29.[30] Her band then performed at the Thurston County Fair in Walthill, Nebraska, on August 30.[31] After this performance, Cora and her new band disappear from the newspapers. It is not known whether they continued to tour, but Cora returned to Tulsa.

Sometime in 1929 or 1930, Cora met a man named Frank Barsanti in Tulsa. Born on August 9, 1895, in Pisa, Italy, Barsanti immigrated to the United States on April 3, 1907, and became a naturalized citizen on January 10, 1919.[32] He moved to Tulsa in 1929 and quickly gained a reputation as a leading turkey grower in eastern Oklahoma.[33] On June 24, 1930, Cora Youngblood Corson married Frank Barsanti.[34] Cora joined him in poultry farming and became co-owner of the Tender Broiler Hatchery.[35] Upon returning home and leaving the newspaper headlines, she appears to have dropped the Princess Youngblood moniker and is only mentioned in connection with Barsanti. In the meantime, Shunatona took his U.S. Indian Reservation Band to perform at "countless national engagements and was featured at the International Exposition in Paris, where it played at the American Building."[36] The band had become a symbol of America's Native culture at the inauguration and now represented a part of the country's identity on an international level.

Just a couple of years later, the 1932 presidential election brought Cora Youngblood Corson, and with her the performance of Princess Youngblood, out of retirement for another stint with the U.S. Indian Reservation Band. Against the backdrop of the Great Depression, Franklin D. Roosevelt easily defeated Herbert Hoover, whom many people had blamed for the economic state of the country. On the event of Roosevelt's inauguration, the United States Indian Reservation Band was once again invited to play at the presidential inauguration, alongside the Philadelphia Harmonica Band. Some papers reported that John F. Kroutil, president of the Roosevelt-Garner Club of Oklahoma, sent the Indian Reservation Band to DC for the event.[37] The two groups performed on March 4, 1933, at the inaugural ball as "twin musical attractions."[38] The tradition of having a charity ball had been broken by President Woodrow Wilson but was now revived under Roosevelt. The papers noted that members of the band, namely Chief Roaring Thunder and

Princess Youngblood, would be on hand for this performance, as they had been four years prior.

This time around, the band was announced to be "made up of 20 full-blooded Indians representing 18 tribes . . . in full Indian regalia" and led by Chief Big Mountain of the Blackfoot tribe.[39] The papers also mentioned that "all the members of this band are university or college graduates and many of them have studied abroad."[40] The newspapers had finally mentioned the education and success of the performers rather than just their outfits. The *Washington Post* provided an interesting look at these two bands, stating that "representatives of families who can trace their lineage several centuries back of the Mayflower invasion will vie with first generation Americans in providing music for the inaugural ball."[41] As in 1929, Cora and the other members of the band represented the Native side of the American identity on a national level.

Due to her past popularity, Cora quickly became the topic of the papers when discussing the Indian Reservation Band. The *Cincinnati Enquirer* noted, "The matter of the Indian Reservation Band is not one to be dismissed lightly, for in that band is Princess Youngblood. Most of the time she runs a chicken ranch in Oklahoma but just let an inauguration or a parade come along, and the Princess quits chicken ranching and plays the tuba."[42] The papers also stated as fact that Cora "is a full-blooded Cherokee and plays the largest tuba in the world."[43] Her successful ethnic impersonation of a Native woman at this national level successfully convinced the press of her false Native heritage.

This time around, Cora's popularity led to interviews with local papers and radio stations. However, one interview revealed Cora's new image with bewildering statements that seemed intended to enhance her "Indianness." The article began with a discussion of her ability and of her "gold tuba" that had traveled with her all over war zones in the world war. "In fact, that tuba has three gold patches" because "it was hit in air raids." The article explained that Cora grew up in Oklahoma and "loves her prairies too much to leave them very often." She would occasionally play with the Indian band but spent most of her time overseeing "the four farms she owns." Cora also told the reporter some of her "most vivid childhood memories about Geronimo, the famous Apache chieftain" to authenticate her new heritage.

> We'd watch him coming down the street and beg him for a story. He was a very old, wrinkled man and very kind. Indians are noted for their kindness to children, you know. If he had some change, he would buy us candy and then tell us stories. His favorite one was about his war blanket. It had 19 scalps attached to it. But to be a true war blanket it should have had 20. Poor Geronimo! He felt so badly that he didn't have that twentieth scalp which would have meant honor to him according to his ancient philosophy.

The article also mentioned that Cora would be wearing "the dress of her ancestors—soft buckskins trimmed with fringe and beads" at the inaugural ball.[44] The dress in question still survives, in my possession. It is secured by snap buttons on both the dress and moccasins, like a costume, confirming that her presentation as a Native woman was an act. Cora was also interviewed by the Greater National Capital Committee as part of a national radio broadcast. They asked Princess Youngblood, a "well-known Cherokee Indian," to describe her reactions to Washington on the eve of the inauguration.[45]

These stories demonstrate Cora's attempt at ethnic impersonation but also highlight her failure in using her knowledge and experiences with Native people in Oklahoma. There are several issues with her statements. For example, Geronimo lived as a prisoner of war at Fort Sill, some forty miles south of Anadarko, from 1894 until his death in 1909. Cora was attempting to cement her fraudulent Native heritage with anecdotes that hark back to her imaginary youth on an "Indian reservation."

At the inaugural ball, the U.S. Indian Reservation Band performed to a crowd of almost 8,200. Unfortunately, President Franklin Roosevelt did not attend, but the first lady, Eleanor Roosevelt, did. The band performed well, but only Cora received special mention in the papers, for being the only woman and having "aroused much interest with her playing of the largest tuba used in any such organization."[46] The band received praise for being "the most interesting" of the performances due to its ability and regalia.[47] After the inauguration, the United States Indian Reservation Band continued to perform at theaters in the Northeast. However, it is not clear whether Cora continued with the band or returned to Oklahoma after the inaugural performance. Regardless, this became Cora's final major performance. She is absent from the papers for the next decade, except with regard to her farming enterprise. After her final work as a performer, Cora returned to retired life and began to raise quail as a hobby. However, she quickly became so successful that Barsanti took the operation over and formed a business. He built specialized cages for the birds and raised six hundred of them in 1935.[48]

This is not to say that Cora's musical career had been forgotten. To the contrary, a 1938 article in the *Tribune* of Scranton, Pennsylvania, contained a "musical quiz" by Dr. D. E. Jones. He asked the reader, "Who was the Indian girl who sang in a Scranton Concert?" The answer: "Cora Youngblood Corson, young Indian soprano, was soloist with the United States Ladies' Military Band at Luna Park, August 4, 1907. After singing several songs, Miss Corson played instrumental solos on the euphonium and bass tuba."[49] This shows Cora's ability to convince her audience of her false Native heritage and speaks to the public's obsession with Native performers as rare commodities. Her performance remained in public memory twenty-one years later.

As Cora continued raising her quail, rumblings on the other side of the world would soon thrust her back into the world of entertainment. Throughout the 1930s, Nazi Germany and Imperial Japan made aggressive moves to expand their national powers. On September 1, 1939, Germany invaded Poland, starting another world war, which would last for the next six years. Recalling the horrors of World War I and the failure of the Treaty of Versailles, America maintained a neutral stance. It did not want to intervene in another European war.

On December 7, 1941, this neutrality was shattered when the Japan launched a surprise attack on the United States naval station at Pearl Harbor, Hawaii. This attack killed and wounded thousands of Americans and destroyed or crippled much of the American Pacific Fleet. The next day, the United States declared war on Japan and entered World War II. Angered by this surprise attack, the American people rallied behind the war effort by enlisting or doing what they could to support the troops. Cora, like many others, used her skills to provide entertainment for American soldiers in Oklahoma.

Although she had stopped performing, Cora joined with her brother-in-law, Glenn Condon, as the first woman involved in the work of Hey Rube, Inc., "a non-profit organization of civilians whose function is to present entertainment for civilian defense workers and soldiers in army camps." Created in 1942, the organization quickly grew from organizing "mainly lines of dancing girls" to

Cora Youngblood Corson (*right*), Glenn Condon (*second from right*), and other members of Hey Rube, Inc. 1943.
Courtesy of the Museum of Tulsa History.

establishing a regular lineup of acts.[50] The group soon attached itself to Camp Gruber near Braggs, Oklahoma, and continued to entertain the camp until the end of the war.[51]

Cora was interviewed by the *Tulsa Tribune* about her experiences with the previous world war. She commented "War? Yes, I know war. It isn't nice. To see all those young men one day playing and laughing and singing as though they hadn't a care in the world, and to see them dead, the next!" The article said she had been "one of the world's most famous entertainers in the early part of the century." She pointed to a dented sousaphone, saying, "We were playing in London in '18 when this happened. The theater had a glass roof, and we were just leaving the stage to play beneath the first balcony when a burst of shrapnel was hurled through the roof." Inexplicably, perhaps as a result of the nature of show business and the created life she had made, the article contains many incorrect details about Cora's life, such as the statements "At 10 she was in her father's band at Anadarko, Ok. At 14 she was a member of Miss Ruth Mae Butler's United States Ladies' band. In 1905 she had formed her own 30-piece band" and "At war's end, the band was booked into South America and Australia, but ships were too crowded, and the band returned to America."[52]

Unfortunately, a year after this interview, Cora took ill, and after a two-week illness she died on July 12, 1943, at the age of fifty-seven, in the home of her sister Eula Condon.[53] She is buried in Rose Hill Memorial Park in Tulsa. Frank Barsanti remarried and moved to Skiatook, Oklahoma, where he died on August 22, 1950, following a cerebral hemorrhage while attending a theater.[54] He is buried in Memorial Park Cemetery in Tulsa.

Following her death, obituaries attempted to capture Cora's life in a brief description. The *Billboard* acknowledged her achievements, such as holding "the only honorary life membership in [the] Actor's Equity Association ever awarded [to] a woman." It also stated that she "won fame as the only woman ever to play triple-tongue solos on the tuba and won competitions on the Scotch bagpipes."[55] The *Tulsa Daily World* noted that her death came "on the eve of the annual reunion of the Rainbow Division Veterans association in Tulsa," which "remembered her well for the many hours of entertainment she provided for them 25 years ago in France and occupied Germany."[56]

However, like the 1942 interview, these pieces also inexplicably contain incorrect information, furthering the mystery of Cora's life. One such claim appeared in the *Billboard* obituary, which stated, "Mrs. Barsanti began her professional career as conductor of a woman's band at the St. Louis World Fair."[57] The *Tulsa Daily World* claimed that Cora had performed at the funeral of President William McKinley and at the inauguration of President Warren G. Harding. It also incorrectly explained that she had "entertained President Woodrow Wilson at his own request" during World War I.[58] These inconsistencies could be attributed to the nature of her career, in which she created her image through her various performances. Regardless, the full life of an influential woman is difficult to surmise without the ability to see the full scope of her impact.

EIGHT

LEGACY

After her death, Cora Youngblood Corson's story started to fade into obscurity. Beyond her family, no one seemed to remember the achievements she had accomplished in her life. Before my research began, Cora only appeared in obscure references in a few books, and only one book mentioned her in any detail. M. Alison Kibler's *Rank Ladies: Gender and Cultural Hierarchy in American Vaudeville* does mention Cora's leadership in the Oklahoma City strike, calling her "the most prominent, outspoken female labor activist for the vaudevillians' cause."[1]

Fortunately, since 2020, Cora has begun to garner the recognition she deserves. Dr. Douglas Yeo created an entry for Cora in his 2021 *An Illustrated Dictionary for the Modern Trombone, Tuba, and Euphonium Player.* In the summer of 2021, I published a short article on Cora's life in the *International Tuba and Euphonium Association Journal.* In 2022, the International Women's Brass Conference recognized Cora with its Pioneer Award for "women who have been pioneers in the top levels of brass performance, breaking down barriers and living their lives effecting change for those who have followed. Each awardee's career and spirit exemplify the goals and traditions of the

IWBC."[2] The unfortunate reality of Cora's obscurity is beginning to fade, and with it her true legacy is being revealed.

Cora was a superb tuba and euphonium player, organizer of musical groups, union activist, and much more. During her career, she inspired women across the country to take up brass instruments by actively speaking out and encouraging new musicians. Cora graced the covers of *Vanity Fair, Variety, Player, Billboard,* and *Performer* magazines multiple times, showcasing her status as an influential musician both nationally and internationally. She became a recognized celebrity and a symbol for the state of Oklahoma. Her fight against the Vaudeville Managers Protective Association made her a recognized union leader, while her performances in Oklahoma gave rural communities the opportunity to view a level of talent that previously had been seen only in the major theaters. For more than twenty years, the C. G. Conn Company used her image and stories to help sell their variety of brass instruments. During her almost thirty-year career, Cora became one of the most famous musicians in the country, creating a new image of what a brass musician could be and achieve.

But the real legacy she left behind is the importance of her success and career to new generations of female brass musicians. Dr. Joanna Ross Hersey, a tubist, performing artist, composer, United States Coast Guard veteran, associate dean of student success, and professor of music at the University of North Carolina at Pembroke, has worked on the history of female tuba players. Hersey's comments on Cora's legacy perhaps best encapsulate the significance of her life:

> Well, to me, she is unique, because even today it feels rare to see a woman making a good professional living with the tuba. I think the scholarship you would do about women tuba players of the past is important because without it women today feel like they're the first. They don't know about the Coras. And it's sort of a social justice thing to me, that these women existed, but there were so many other men that they just got buried under all of it and it's not common to know about them. So, when a girl hauls a tuba around in 2024, everybody is shocked and amazed. And it wears on her, and they are leaving the field . . . If you look at the stats, there's a lot of women taking up tuba as girls, and during the collegiate years, but it doesn't trickle into the professional setting, because I think it's just too difficult, and they're

> not willing to do it, because everybody's so shocked all the time. There are certainly more than there were years ago; we can all point to several women teaching tuba at the collegiate level now. But overall, if you ask us, we all say that everywhere we go people are surprised and make a comment about a woman and her tuba or whatever . . . To see a role model like Cora celebrated is to fill in the gaps of history, people who genuinely were breaking barriers.[3]

Cora Youngblood Corson defied all social conventions and succeeded against seemingly insurmountable odds. She laid the groundwork for generations of women musicians and proved that the long-held beliefs about the place of women in music and vaudeville could be challenged and overcome.

EPILOGUE

Meet the Band

Cora's success did not rely solely on her own skills. Over almost twenty years, many women played in the various iterations of her band. Every one of these women was an expert musician on her instrument and deserves to have some recognition for the part she played in pioneering the field. Unfortunately, many of their names are missing from historical records, as are the dates they performed with Cora. Any exclusion is not purposeful but rather a reflection of lack of information.

Eleanor Graycia Acton. Born in Ulysses, Nebraska, on March 27, 1885. Her family moved to Anadarko, Oklahoma, before 1900. In 1901, she worked as one of the first telephone operators in Anadarko. One of Cora's longest friends, she joined the Ladies Cornet Band in 1902, playing trombone, and continued until the end of Cora's musical career in 1928. She married Kenneth Cecil Kruger on June 14, 1938. She died on September 9, 1956, in El Reno, Oklahoma.

Hattie Deane Acton. Born in Benedict, Nebraska, on March 11, 1890. She played with Cora from 1913 to 1917. She married William J. Vann on December 1, 1917. She died on February 2, 1975.

Anna Bell Alkire. Born in Wood Corners, Wisconsin, on May 14, 1889. After graduating high school, she attended the Minneapolis School of Music and then Dana's Musical Institute in Warren, Ohio. She then toured with Cora. She later married Henry T. Fox on October 4, 1927. She died on March 2, 1938, in Durand, Wisconsin.[1]

Florence Baird. She played baritone in the Ladies Cornet Band from 1902 to 1903. She also performed in the Oklahoma Press Association Band at the 1904 St. Louis World's Fair.

Kathleen Ballinger. She performed with Cora in 1924.

Emily Ann Sloan Bickford. Born in Superior, Wisconsin, in 1907. As a young child she took drum lessons. In junior high she took up the trombone. In 1925, at the age of eighteen, she joined Cora's band. She died at the age of fifty-six.

Bunnie Cleveland. She played the cornet in the Ladies Cornet Band from 1902 to 1903.

Eunice Cleveland. She played the French horn in the Ladies Cornet Band from 1902 to 1903. She married D. E. Oldsburg on March 21, 1908.

Iona Cooley. She played the French horn in the Ladies Cornet Band from 1902 to 1903. She married W. P. Cooper on November 24, 1904.

Della Cozine. She performed with Cora from 1922 to 1925.

Gladys Barbara Cronk. Born in Rockland, Wisconsin, on January 11, 1898. She performed in the Montfort Girls' Band in Montfort, Wisconsin, before joining Cora's band. She played cornet and trombone with Cora from 1913 to 1925. She died on July 3, 1987, in Chicago, Illinois.

Lou Daniels. She played the French horn in the Ladies Cornet Band from 1902 to 1903. She then became a teacher. She married Martin Rolette on June 30, 1908.

Clairette Marie Hamel. Born in Montreal, Canada, on October 26, 1899. She performed with Cora during the war, from 1917 to 1919. She married William Gallant on October 11, 1939. She died on May 14, 1962, in Windsor, Ontario.

Simone Hamel. She performed for Cora along with her sister Clairette during the war, from 1917 to 1919.

Ruth Wanda Hart. Born in Lafayette, Indiana, on October 14, 1908. She played the cornet, trombone, and banjo and sang in Cora's band in the mid-1920s.[2] She later married Wilbur Budd Hulick, of Stoopnagle and Budd, a popular radio comedy team in the 1930s, on November 10, 1930. She died on February 16, 1978, in Escondido, California.

Ethel Mary Hiatt. Born in Claytonville, Illinois, on June 25, 1889. She grew up in a musical family and began music lessons at an early age. She played trumpet, violin, clarinet, saxophone, and drums. She originally traveled with her family as part of the Hiatt Family Orchestra. She had joined Cora's band by 1914 and played at least through 1919. She married Ervin Renegar on November 6, 1928. She then became a music teacher. She died on June 1, 1976, in Newcastle, Indiana.

Olive Annice Hiatt. Born in Newcastle, Indiana, on May 18, 1899. She grew up in a musical family and began music lessons at an early age. She played with her family as part of the Hiatt Family Orchestra and then with Cora in 1917, performing with her overseas. She married Herbert Poston on June 24, 1922. She died on November 19, 1990, in Newcastle, Indiana.

Ethel Hoagland. She played the baritone in the Ladies Cornet Band from 1902 to 1903. She married Charles J. Wheeler on October 22, 1902.

Nora Johnson. She played the snare drum in the Ladies Cornet Band from 1902 to 1903.

Daisy Kane. She played the cornet in the Ladies Cornet Band from 1902 to 1903.

Mrs. G. W. Keeler. Possibly Agnes Blanche Beydler, who married George W. Keeler. She played bass drum in the Ladies Cornet Band from 1902 to 1903.

Nellie C. Kennedy. She played the bass drum in the Ladies Cornet Band from 1902 to 1903. She later attended the University of Kansas in Lawrence.

Lois Land. She appeared on the cover of *Variety* alongside other sextet members in 1913.

Lonna Lewis. She performed with Cora in 1925.

Maggie Lober. She joined the Ladies Cornet Band in 1902.

Mae McBride. Born in Mystic, Connecticut, on November 23, 1890. She played trombone in Cora's band from 1912 to 1917, when she married Cora's brother, Isaac Youngblood. She died on September 24, 1968, in Tulsa, Oklahoma. She is also my great-great-grandmother.

Ida Mae Mundell. Born in Chickasha, Oklahoma, on November 18, 1886. Her family moved to Anadarko, Oklahoma, before 1900. In 1901, she worked as one of the first telephone operators in Anadarko. One of Cora's longest friends, she joined the Ladies Cornet Band in 1902, playing trombone, baritone, and cornet until 1919, when she married Patrick J. Burke. She died on January 5, 1951, in Los Angeles, California.

Lela Marie Myers. Born in Capioma, Kansas, on October 25, 1897. She traveled overseas with Cora during World War I, from 1917 to 1919. She later married James Alexander McRoberts on March 21, 1921. She died on June 8, 1971, in Merriam, Kansas.

Helen Palmer. She was from Kansas and played with Cora from 1924 to 1925.

Maggie Smith. She played clarinet in the Ladies Cornet Band from 1902 to 1903. She married B. G. Hoosier on October 7, 1904.

Lilly Taylor. She performed with Cora in 1924.

Ethel Maude Wright. Born in Melrose, Massachusetts, on August 5, 1895. She began playing the cornet at age seven as a pupil of Godfrey McMullin. She toured with Cora before later marrying William H. Kelley. She died on June 2, 1976.

Mae Wright. She performed with Cora from 1914 to 1916.

Beulah Young. She played baritone in the Ladies Cornet Band from 1902 to 1903.

Winnie Young. She played trombone in the Ladies Cornet Band from 1902 to 1903.

Corrine Ruth Youngblood. Born in Oklahoma on September 2, 1907. She was Cora's niece. She performed with Cora in 1925.

Eula Youngblood. Born in Republic, Missouri, on June 14, 1893. Cora's sister. Joined Cora in the Ladies Cornet Band in 1902 and played until she married Glenn Condon on June 15, 1913. She died on March 7, 1965, in Tulsa, Oklahoma.

Jimmie Youngblood. Likely a nickname. I am unable to determine who Jimmie was, but she performed with Cora in 1925.

NOTES

INTRODUCTION

1. Berkhofer, *White Man's Indian*, 95–101.

2. Deloria, *Playing Indian*, 7.

3. Trachtenberg, *Shades of Hiawatha*, 170.

4. Bird, *Dressing in Feathers*, 7, 11.

5. Deloria, *Indians in Unexpected Places*, 6, 57–58.

6. Bold, *"Vaudeville Indians,"* 41.

7. "Vaudeville Actors' Haven," *Billboard*, August 7, 1920, 20.

1. HUMBLE BEGINNINGS

1. Smith, *Republic, Missouri*, 2.

2. Quaife, *Jeremiah Youngblood*, 667.

3. "A Lustful Beast," *Sedalia (MO) Democrat*, March 18, 1894, 5.

4. "Tulsa Woman Played for the Boys 'Over There,'" *Tulsa (OK) Tribune*, January 3, 1942.

5. "Water Lilies," *St. Louis (MO) Post-Dispatch*, September 14, 1901.

6. Riffel and Bell, "Anadarko."

7. "Town Lots Sold: August 6, 1901," unpublished, Anadarko Philomathic Museum, Oklahoma.

8. "J. M. Youngblood," advertisement, *Evening Tribune*, Anadarko, OK, September 26, 1901.

9. "Trade with J M Youngblood," advertisement, *Daily Democrat*, Anadarko, OK, January 30, 1902; "Your Photo Enlarged Free," advertisement, *Caddo County Times*, Anadarko, OK, February 6, 1902.

10. "Just Received!," advertisement, *Caddo County Times*, Anadarko, OK, July 24, 1902.

11. "Local Items," advertisement, *Anadarko (OK) Evening Tribune*, August 25, 1902.

12. "The People Will Go Where They Can Do the Best," *Week's Review*, Anadarko, OK, December 13, 1902.

13. "Oh Music Sweet Music," advertisement, *Daily Democrat,* Anadarko, OK, September 11, 1905.

14. See Polito, *Savage Art,* 29.

15. "Isn't It the Biggest Baby That Your Ever Saw?," *Anadarko (OK) Daily Democrat,* August 5, 1902, 1.

16. Sullivan, *Women's Bands in America,* 2–3.

17. Howe, "Town Bands, 1880–1920," 51–53.

18. "Eighteen of Anadarko's Brightest," *Anadarko (OK) Daily Democrat,* August 14, 1902.

19. "A Paper Is Being Circulated," *Anadarko (OK) Evening Tribune,* August 15, 1902.

20. "The Ladies Band," *Caddo County Times,* Anadarko, OK, January 1, 1903.

21. "Notice," *Anadarko (OK) Evening Tribune,* September 29, 1902.

22. "Program," *Daily Democrat,* Anadarko, OK, September 17, 1902.

23. "Ladies' Band," *Anadarko (OK) Evening Tribune,* October 13, 1902.

24. "Another Band," *Anadarko (OK) Evening Tribune,* October 25, 1902.

25. "Charles Corson Student Information Card," RG 75, series 1329, box 1, National Archives and Records Administration, available at Carlisle Indian School Digital Resource Center, https://carlisleindian.dickinson.edu/student_files/charles-corson-student-information-card.carlisleindian.dickinson.edu.

26. "The Following Musicians," *Indian Helper,* Carlisle, PA, December 1, 1899.

27. "The Blacksmith–Tailor Game Tomorrow," *Red Man and Helper,* Carlisle, PA, November 22, 1901.

28. "Charles Corson," *Red Man and Helper,* Carlisle, PA, January 17, 1902.

29. "From Mark Penoi '98 and Charles Corson 1900, jointly, who are Employed at Anadarko, Oklahoma," *Red Man and Helper,* Carlisle, PA, March 4, 1902.

30. "Corson and Penoi," *Red Man and Helper,* Carlisle, PA, November 21, 1902.

31. "Tony the Convict," *Anadarko (OK) Evening Tribune,* October 18, 1902.

32. "A Grand Success," *Anadarko (OK) Evening Tribune,* October 27, 1902.

33. "Tony the Convict," *Anadarko (OK) Evening Tribune,* October 28, 1902.

34. "One Dollar Better," *Anadarko (OK) Evening Tribune,* October 21, 1902.

35. "The Band," *Daily Democrat,* Anadarko, OK, October 22, 1902.

36. "'C' Street to the Front," *Daily Democrat,* Anadarko, OK, October 23, 1902.

37. "Down at Anadarko," *Anadarko (OK) Tribune,* October 31, 1902.

38. "Karl Preger the Lucky Man," *Daily Democrat,* Anadarko, OK, October 25, 1902.

39. "The Big Rally a Success," *Daily Democrat,* Anadarko, OK, November 3, 1902.

40. "The Anadarko Ladies," *Anadarko (OK) Tribune,* November 14, 1902.

41. "Minister's Family Serenaded," *Anadarko (OK) Daily Democrat,* December 6, 1902.

42. "The Ladies Band," *Caddo County Times,* Anadarko, OK, December 11, 1902.

43. "Enthusiasm Prevails," *Anadarko (OK) Tribune,* January 2, 1903; "Woodman Banquet," *Daily Democrat,* Anadarko, OK, January 6, 1903.

44. "Ladies Band Concert," *Anadarko (OK) Daily Democrat,* January 9, 1903.

45. "As a friend . . . ," editorial, *Daily Democrat,* Anadarko, OK, January 13, 1903.

46. "Hon. W. J. Bryan," *Anadarko (OK) Daily Democrat,* January 12 and 15, 1903.

47. "A Visit to Anadarko," letter, *Anadarko (OK) Daily Democrat,* February 3, 1903.

48. "Prof. Segar," *Daily Democrat,* Anadarko, OK, February 11, 1903.

49. "Lawton Ladies Band," *Daily Democrat,* Anadarko, OK, February 13, 1903.

50. "To Organize Ladies Band," *Lawton (OK) News,* April 9, 1903.

51. "Mr. Charles Corson and Miss Cora Youngblood," *Anadarko (OK) Daily Democrat,* April 27, 1903.

52. Jim Smith, *Republic, Missouri,* 134.

53. Parezo and Fowler, *Anthropology Goes to the Fair,* 1.

54. Gilbert, *Whose Fair,* 4.

55. Debo, *Geronimo,* 1996.

56. Parezo and Fowler, *Anthropology Goes to the Fair,* 112.

57. Ibid., 113–114.

58. Deloria, *Indians in Unexpected Places,* 136.

59. Parezo and Fowler, *Anthropology Goes to the Fair,* 2.

60. "The Oklahoma World's Fair Association," *Lawton (OK) News-Republican,* March 31, 1904, 8.

61. "Oklahoma at the World's Fair," *Pythian Times,* Perry, OK, January 1, 1904, 1.

62. Parezo and Fowler, *Anthropology Goes to the Fair,* 2.

63. "How Guthrie Got There," *Oklahoma State Capital,* Guthrie, May 26, 1904.

64. "Some of the Members," *Edmond (OK) Enterprise and Oklahoma County News,* April 28, 1904; "Off to St. Louis," *Daily Democrat,* Anadarko, OK, May 12, 1904.

65. "Ladies' Band," *Lawton (OK) Constitution,* June 2, 1904.

66. "Sights and Echoes at the Exposition," *St. Louis (MO) Globe-Democrat,* May 17, 1904.

67. "Editors of the World," *Chandler Publicist,* May 20, 1904; "Oklahoma Press Association," *Helena Herald,* May 20, 1904; "How Guthrie Got There."

68. Schwartz, *Bands at the St. Louis World's Fair of 1904,* 46; "How Guthrie Got There."

69. Hauptman and McLester, *Oneida Indians in the Age of Allotment,* 112–13.

70. Schwartz, *Bands at the St. Louis World's Fair of 1904,* 7; *Daily Official Program,* June 17, 1904, 13.

71. "Married at the Fair," *Anaconda (MT) Standard,* June 29, 1904.

72. "Mrs. Cora Corson," *Plain Dealer,* Anadarko, OK, August 4, 1904.

73. Letter from Schuler Corson to Charles Corson, November 24, 1904, author's collection.

2. THE RISE

1. "Sign a Ladies' Band," advertisement, *Iola (KS) Daily Record,* June 4, 1906, 2.

2. Meyers, "Helen May Butler and Her Ladies' Military Band," 15–20.

3. Ibid., 20–25.

4. "An Oklahoma Musician," *Daily Oklahoman,* Oklahoma City, October 3, 1905.

5. "Another Indian Musician," *Wichita (KS) Eagle,* July 13, 1906.

6. "An Oklahoma Musician."

7. "The Ladies Band," *Gadsden (AL) Daily Times-News,* October 20, 1905; "Ladies' Band Well Received," *Chattanooga News,* October 23, 1905.

8. "For Gahagan Rifles," *Chattanooga (TN) Daily Times,* November 29, 1905.

9. "Ladies' Band Closes," *Billboard,* December 30, 1905, 2.

10. "Ladies' Military Band," *Birmingham (AL) News,* April 28, 1906.

11. "Vaudeville," *Billboard,* September 8, 1906, 28.

12. "Star Theater," *Atlanta (GA) Constitution,* January 28, 1906.

13. "Mrs. Carson's Wonderful Success," *Daily Democrat,* Anadarko, OK, February 22, 1906.

14. Bold, *"Vaudeville Indians,"* 50.

15. Hersey, "An Attraction of Unusual Merit," 74.

16. "Helen May Butler," advertisement, *Billboard,* March 17, 1906, 63.

17. "Cora Youngblood Corson," *San Antonio (TX) Sunday Light,* April 1, 1906.

18. "Two Concerts Given Today for San Francisco Victims," *Atlanta (GA) Constitution,* April 22, 1906.

19. "Sacred Concert to Be Given at East Lake," *Birmingham (AL) News,* April 27, 1906.

20. "Ladies' Military Band."

21. "Helen Butler's Band," advertisement, *Age-Herald,* Birmingham, AL, April 29, 1906.

22. "Next Week at Forest Park," *Arkansas Democrat,* Little Rock, May 27, 1906.

23. "Amusements," *Daily Arkansas Gazette,* Little Rock, May 31, 1906.

24. "Bring $1,000 Feature," *Iola (KS) Daily Register and Evening News,* June 4, 1906; "Sign a Ladies' Band."

25. "Electric Park Features," *Fort Smith Times,* Arkansas, June 10, 1906.

26. "Fourth of July," *Wichita (KS) Beacon,* July 3, 1906, 6.

27. "Helen May Butler's Band," *Wichita (KS) Daily Eagle,* July 1, 1906.

28. "At Wonderland Park," *Wichita (KS) Daily Eagle,* July 4, 1906.

29. "Fourth of July at Wonderland Park," *Wichita (KS) Beacon,* July 3, 1906.

30. "At Wonderland Park."

31. Jeff Chapman, "Delmar Garden Theater," *Cinema Treasures,* http://cinematreasures.org/theaters/16488.

32. "Season of 1906," *Daily Oklahoman,* Oklahoma City, May 6, 1906.

33. "Miss Cora Youngblood Corson," advertisement, *St. Joseph (MO) News-Press/Gazette,* July 13, 1906.

34. "Secure More Bands," *Daily Times,* Dubuque, IA, July 8, 1906.

35. "Young Indian Girl with Butler's Band," *Dubuque (IA) Telegraph-Herald,* July 22, 1906.

36. Troutman, "Joe Shunatona and the United States Indian Reservation Orchestra," 17.

37. Deloria, *Indians in Unexpected Places,* 188.

38. Phillips, *Staging Indigeneity,* 12.

39. "The People, The Place."

40. "Ladies' Band Is Given an Ovation," *Dubuque (IA) Telegraph-Herald,* July 30, 1906.

41. "Banner Night at Union Park," *Dubuque (IA) Telegraph-Herald,* August 2, 1906.

42. "Good One on the Indian Girl," *Dubuque (IA) Telegraph-Herald,* August 3, 1906.

43. "Performer Dates," *Billboard,* August 11, 1906, 20.

44. "Cora Youngblood Corson," *Billboard,* August 4, 1906, 8.

45. "Secure More Bands."

46. "Vaudeville," *Billboard,* September 8, 1906, 28.

47. "The Chief Feature . . . ," *Des Moines (IA) Register,* October 7, 1906; "Playhouses and Players," *Des Moines Register,* October 9, 1906.

48. "Vaudeville," *Billboard,* November 3, 1906, 11.

49. "Vaudeville," *Billboard,* November 24, 1906, 46.

50. "New Elite Theater Ready to Open," *Rock Island (IL) Argus,* December 22, 1906; "Elite's Seats Have Arrived," *Rock Island Argus,* December 28, 1906.

51. On gender stereotypes and brass instruments, see Scherer, "Top Brass," 63; and Cumberledge, "Instrument and Gender."

52. Maclead, "Whence Comes the Lady Timpanist?," 294.

53. W. J. Henderson, "Music and Musicians," *New York Sun,* November 16, 1935, 9.

54. *Musical Standard,* April 2, 1904, cited in Green, *Music, Gender, Education,* 67.

55. "Miss Cora Youngblood Corson," *Logansport (IN) Journal,* March 24, 1907.

56. "Miss Grace Acton," *Chickasha (OK) Daily Express,* May 10, 1907.

57. "White City," *Kentucky Irish American,* Louisville, June 8, 1907.

58. "Cora Youngblood Corson's Women's Band White City's Star Attraction," *Courier-Journal,* Louisville, KY, June 9, 1907.

59. "Revolutionary Changes Noted at the White City," *Courier-Journal,* Louisville, KY, June 12, 1907.

60. "Cora Youngblood Carson's Women's Band at White City This Week Again," *Courier-Journal,* Louisville, KY, June 16, 1907.

61. "Big Crowds," *Courier-Journal,* Louisville, KY, June 17, 1907.

62. "Amusements," *Scranton (PA) Republican,* August 3 and August 5, 1907.

63. "Amusements," *Scranton (PA) Republican,* August 4, 1907.

64. "Ladies' Band Scores a Hit a Luna Park," *Scranton (PA) Republican,* August 5, 1907, 6.

65. "Ladies Band at Luna Park," *Scranton (PA) Truth,* August 5, 1907.

66. "Ladies Band Scores a Hit at Luna Park."

67. "Amusements," *Scranton (PA) Republican,* August 6, 1907.

68. "Excellent Music," *Detroit Free Press,* August 16, 1907.

69. "United States Ladies Military Band," *Daily Herald,* Port Huron, MI, August 23, 1907.

70. "Our Beautiful Dark-Eyed Anna," *Anadarko (OK) Evening Tribune,* August 12, 1902, 2.

3. VAUDEVILLE

1. Hersey, "An Attraction of Unusual Merit," 74–75.

2. Bold, *"Vaudeville Indians,"* 3.

3. Deloria, *Indians in Unexpected Places,* 211–12.

4. "Cora Youngblood Corson," *Billboard,* September 29, 1907, 6.

5. "Cora Youngblood Corson," *Variety,* October 26, 1907, 6.

6. "Good Bill at Majestic," *Wisconsin State Journal,* Madison, October 15, 1907.

7. "A Bill of Large Proportions . . . ," *Morning News,* Wilmington, DE, January 6, 1908.

8. "The Many Patrons . . . ," *Morning News,* Wilmington, DE, January 3, 1908.

9. "Cora Youngblood Corson," *Evening Journal,* Wilmington, DE, January 6, 1908.

10. "Plays Last Night," *Morning News,* Wilmington, DE, January 7, 1908.

11. "Observations of the Stroller on Theatrical Life and Environment," *Billboard,* July 11, 1908.

12. "Large Crowds," *Courier-Journal,* Louisville, KY, July 12, 1908.

13. "Music, Drama, Parks," *Indianapolis (IN) Star,* August 18, 1908.

14. "Observations of the Stroller on Theatrical Life and Environment," *Billboard,* December 5, 1908.

15. Ibid.

16. "Cora Youngblood Corson," *Billboard,* October 17, 1908, 41.

17. "Montauk Theatre, Passaic," *Passaic (NJ) Daily Herald,* March 19, 1909.

18. "Word Has Been Received," *Daily Democrat,* Anadarko, OK, March 11, 1909.

19. "Big Bill at the Bay," *Daily Record,* Long Branch, NJ, July 9, 1909.

20. "Next Week at the Savoy," *Fall River (MA) Herald,* November 27, 1909.

21. "Secure More Bands."

22. "The Scenic," *Hartford (CT) Courant,* December 14, 1909.

23. "Too Much Lung Expansion," *Variety,* October 2, 1909, 9.

24. "Cora Youngblood Corson," *Kalamazoo (MI) Gazette,* June 1, 1910.

25. "Observations of the Stroller," *Billboard,* October 8, 1910, 15.

26. "$10,000 Beauty Instrument," postcard, author's collection.

27. "Cora Youngblood Corson," *Kalamazoo Gazette.*

28. Lewis, [Sam M.] and [Leo] Bennett, "Cowboy, Nowboy," musical score (Joseph W. Stern, 1909).

29. Meyer, "Helen May Butler and Her Ladies' Military Band," 24.

30. "Chicago Variety Bills," *Billboard,* May 7, 1910, 9.

31. "Miss Grace Acton . . . ," *Anadarko (OK) Tribune,* July 21, 1910; "Family Reunion and Picnic," *Anadarko (OK) Tribune,* September 1, 1910.

32. "New Theater," *Baltimore (MD) Sun,* May 14, 1911.

33. "The Folly," *Daily Oklahoman,* Oklahoma City, September 30, 1910.

34. "Foll," *Daily Oklahoman,* Oklahoma City, October 6, 1910.

35. "Grand Theater Bill Is Exceptionally Classy," *Joliet (IL) Evening Herald-News,* November 13, 1910.

36. "Theater Talk," *News-Journal,* Mansfield, OH, March 28, 1911.

37. "Cora Youngblood Sextette," *Hamilton (OH) Evening Journal,* April 14, 1911.

38. "Slater Theatre," *Pottsville (PA) Republican,* November 17, 1911.

39. "Big Act Tonight," *Evening Capital,* Annapolis, MD, April 8, 1912.

40. "Tribute of Appreciation," *Evening Capital,* Annapolis, MD, April 13, 1912.

41. "An All Girl Cast," *Evening Capital,* Annapolis, MD, February 29, 1912.

42. "Sherbrooke Fair," *Vermont Union-Journal,* Lyndonville, August 21, 1912.

43. "Route Book of Mae McBride," author's collection.

44. "Hundredth Anniversary," *Player,* August 30, 1912, 27.

45. "Cora Youngblood Corson," *Variety,* August 30, 1912, 8.

46. "Cora Youngblood Corson," *Billboard,* August 31, 1912, 6.

47. "Anadarko's Own Girls Here to Entertain Us," *Anadarko (OK) American,* December 19, 1912.

48. "Great Feature at the Wonderland," *Tulsa (OK) Daily Democrat,* December 30, 1912.

49. "1913 Arrived on Time in Tulsa," *Morning Tulsa (OK) Daily World,* January 1, 1913, 5.

50. "Today's Amusements," *Tulsa (OK) Daily World,* January 1, 1913, 8.

51. "Amusements," *Pine Bluff (AR) Daily Graphic,* January 5, 1913, 7.

52. "The Majestic," *Shreveport (LA) Journal,* January 8, 1913, 3; January 10, 1913.

53. "Slater's Great Show," *Pottsville (PA) Daily Republican,* November 25, 1913, 4.

54. "Cora Youngblood Corson's Instrumentalists," *Billboard,* September 12, 1914, 8.

55. "Sextet of Girls Attractive Spot on Pantages Bill," *Spokane (WA) Chronicle,* May 24, 1913, 8.

56. "Weddings in June," *Player,* June 20, 1913, 18.

57. "Cora Youngblood Corson Sextet Champions Wild West," *Player,* May 30, 1913, 6.

58. "At Pantages," *Province,* Vancouver, BC, June 7, 1913, 25.

59. "Pantages Has Topnotcher Program," *Vancouver (BC) Sun,* June 9, 1913, 9.

60. "In Vaudeville," *Missoulian,* Missoula, MT, July 1, 1913, 10.

61. "To Make It a 12-Act," *Player,* July 18, 1913, 22.

62. "Miss Hattie Acton," *Anadarko (OK) Democrat,* July 17, 1913, 5.

63. "Empress," *Tulsa (OK) Daily World,* July 31, 1913, 7.

64. "Stage Girls Have Xmas Tree," *Inter Ocean,* Chicago, IL, December 28, 1913, 42.

65. "Won Prize at Mardi Gras," *Tulsa (OK) Daily World,* February 28, 1914, 7.

66. "Numerous Maskers Attracted to Store at Baronne and Lafayette Streets," *Times-Democrat,* New Orleans, LA, February 25, 1914, 5.

67. "Acton Family Reunion," *Anadarko (OK) Tribune,* June 11, 1914, 5; "Miss Ida Mundell," *Anadarko Tribune,* July 2, 1914, 9.

68. "Mrs. J. M. Youngblood," *Tulsa (OK) Daily World,* August 5, 1914, 3.

69. "Tulsa Again on the Map; Plans for Band," *Tulsa (OK) Daily World,* October 2, 1914, 7.

70. "Vaudeville's Best Farce Comedy Is Coming to Empress," *Fort Wayne (IN) Journal-Gazette,* January 31, 1915, 20; "New Palace," *Star Tribune,* Minneapolis, MN, March 7, 1915, 30.

71. "Cora Youngblood Corson Was a Cow Girl," *Star Tribune,* Minneapolis, MN, March 11, 1915, 9.

72. "Girls From the Golden West to Be Headliner," *Calgary (Alberta) Herald,* April 5, 1915, 5.

73. "Cora Corson Players Will Be Seen Soon," *Spokane (WA) Chronicle,* April 9, 1915, 20.

74. "Pantages," *Seattle (WA) Star,* April 24, 1915, 2.

75. "Cora Corson Players Will Be Seen Soon."

76. "Pantages Has 'Lung' Champion," *Spokesman-Review,* Spokane, WA, April 18, 1915, 29.

77. "Woman Has Unique Scheme for Cure of Tuberculosis," *Seattle (WA) Daily Times,* April 28, 1915, 8.

78. "Oklahoma Girl Is Honored at Frisco," *Tulsa (OK) Daily World,* May 30, 1915.

79. "Oklahoma Girl Is Honored at Frisco," *Morning Tulsa (OK) Daily World,* June 4, 1915, 8.

80. "Friends in This City," *Tulsa (OK) Daily World,* June 2, 1915, 4.

81. "Sousa's Band at C. G. Conn Booth," *Music Trade Review,* June 12, 1915, 12.

82. "Cora and Her Girls Wednesday, July 28th," *American-Democrat,* Anadarko, OK, July 22, 1915, 1.

83. "Instrumentalists Draw Good Crowd," *American-Democrat,* Anadarko, OK, July 29, 1915, 1.

84. "All From Oklahoma," *Tulsa (OK) Daily World,* August 1, 1915.

85. "Corson Band Girls Play for C. of C.," *Tulsa (OK) Daily World,* August 3, 1915, 10.

86. "Cozy Theatre," *Okmulgee (OK) Daily Democrat,* August 9, 1915, 4.

87. "Show at Cozy Is the Big Sensation," *Okmulgee (OK) Daily Democrat,* August 9, 1915, 4.

88. "Film Flashes," *Tulsa (OK) World,* August 22, 1915.

89. "Cora Youngblood Corson," *Billboard,* October 3, 1914, 1.

90. "Fairs Played," advertisement, *Billboard,* November 13, 1915, 64.

4. WAR AT HOME

1. Stewart, *No Applause,* 122–23.

2. Segrave, *Actors Organize,* 30.

3. Slide, *Encyclopedia of Vaudeville,* 554.

4. Haupert, *Entertainment Industry,* 16.

5. "Oklahoma Girl Is Fighting Octopus," *Tulsa (OK) World,* January 5, 1916.

6. "Vaudeville Actors' Haven," August 7, 1920.

7. "Oklahoma Girl Is Fighting Octopus."

8. "She Is Fighting the Vaudeville Trust," *Claremore (OK) Progress and Rogers County Democrat,* January 20, 1916, 7.

9. "Cora Youngblood Corson's Lady Instrumentalists," *Tahlequah (OK) Arrow,* January 22, 1916, 3.

10. "The Cora Youngblood Company," *Vinita (OK) Weekly,* January 27, 1916, 8.

11. "Coming First Half of Next Week," *Morning News,* Coffeyville, KS, January 28, 1916, 1.

12. "Cora Youngblood Corson," *Collinsville (OK) Times,* February 2, 1916, 3.

13. "Well Known Among Noted Musicians," *Collinsville (OK) Weekly News,* February 3, 1916, 1.

14. "W.R.A.U. Contract May Become a Law," *Tulsa (OK) Daily World,* January 28, 1916, 4.

15. "A Loyalist at Last Writes to The Billboard Asking Space," *Billboard,* February 12, 1916, 3, 58, 63.

16. "I'm Fighting the Vaudeville Trust," letter, *McAlester (OK) News-Capital,* February 12, 1916, 3.

17. "Cozy Secures Stellar Attraction," *Kingfisher (OK) Times,* February 17, 1916, 1.

18. "Cora Youngblood Corson Opens Heart to Sing Praises of Her Native State," *Daily Oklahoman,* Oklahoma City, February 20, 1916, 41.

19. "The Southwest VMA," *New York Clipper,* April 22, 1916, 6.

20. "Following a spicy . . . ," *Morning Tulsa (OK) Daily World,* May 16, 1916, 3.

21. "Vaudeville Notes," *Billboard,* June 3, 1916, 17.

22. "Cora Youngblood Corson, Deputy Organizer," *New York Clipper,* June 10, 1916, 3.

23. "Musicians Strike with Stage Hands," *Tulsa (OK) Daily World,* July 21, 1916, 5.

24. "Stage Hands Out, Striking for Pay," *Daily Oklahoman,* Oklahoma City, July 17, 1916, 1.

25. "New Theater After Strike?," *Daily Oklahoman,* Oklahoma City, July 24, 1916, 8.

26. "Theaters Are Picketed," *Daily Oklahoman,* Oklahoma City, July 28, 1916, 16.

27. "Strikers Picket Theaters," *Daily Oklahoman,* Oklahoma City, July 31, 1916, 2.

28. "Newspaper Sues Theater Owners," *Tulsa (OK) Daily World,* August 10, 1916, 1.

29. "Strike Directed at Booking Agencies," *Tulsa (OK) Democrat,* August 11, 1916, 9.

30. "Actor's Strike Will Be Called in Tulsa," *Tulsa (OK) Democrat,* August 11, 1916, 10.

31. "Mountford's Statements Not Borne Out by Facts," *Billboard,* September 2, 1916, 8.

32. "Theater Strike Continues; Employees Winning," *Oklahoma Federationist,* Oklahoma City, August 12, 1916, 1.

33. "White Rat-ism at Stake," *Daily Oklahoman,* Oklahoma City, August 19, 1916, 3.

34. "Artists' Forum," *Variety,* August 11, 1916, 8.

35. "Roughnecks at the Capital," *Evening Times,* Tulsa, OK, August 19, 1916, 4.

36. "Miss Corson Sues Theatrical Heads," *Tulsa (OK) World,* August 16, 1916, 2.

37. Harry Mountford, "The Oklahoma Outburst," *Variety,* August 18, 1916, 14.

38. "Theater Pickets Put Under Arrest," *Morning Tulsa (OK) Daily World,* August 22, 1916, 5.

39. "Theater Pickets Draw Fines of $25," *Morning Tulsa (OK) Daily World,* August 23, 1916, 10.

40. "Unionists Criticize Head of Chamber of Commerce for Anti-Union Sympathy," *Tulsa (OK) Democrat,* August 24, 1916, 1.

41. "Good Bill at Grand Opera House," *St. Louis (MO) Star and Times,* August 23, 1916, 9.

42. Editorial, *Employer,* Oklahoma City, September 1, 1916, 12.

43. "Two Theater Pickets Fined," *Oklahoma City (OK) Times,* September 9, 1916, 1.

44. "Inside Dope of Rat Union May Be Told Board," *Oklahoma News,* Oklahoma City, September 14, 1916, 1.

45. "Arbitration Board Investigates Strike," *Oklahoma Federationist,* Oklahoma City, September 16, 1916, 1; "State Board Is Holding Session on Strike Cause," *Oklahoma Federationist,* September 23, 1916, 1.

46. "Board Submits Findings," *Oklahoma Federationist,* Oklahoma City, September 30, 1916, 1.

47. "Ordinance Is Intolerable," *Oklahoma Federationist,* Oklahoma City, October 14, 1916, 1.

48. "Pickets Again in Front of Shows," *Daily Oklahoman,* Oklahoma City, October 17, 1916, 1.

49. "Ordinance Before High Court," *Oklahoma Federationist,* Oklahoma City, October 21, 1916, 1.

50. "Booking Lockout Effective Today," *Daily Oklahoman,* Oklahoma City, November 1, 1816, 9.

51. Slide, *Encyclopedia of Vaudeville,* 368.

52. "Arson and Violence," *Employer,* Oklahoma City, November 1, 1916, 7.

53. "Harry Mountford—Will You Make Good," *Billboard,* October 21, 1916, 20.

54. "Candidates Have an Eventful Day," *Tulsa (OK) World,* November 4, 1916.

55. "White Rats Get Support of Labor," *Tulsa (OK) Daily World,* November 23, 1916, 4.

56. "West's Letter," *Billboard,* November 4, 1916, 14.

57. "Cora's Self Boosting," *Variety,* November 24, 1916, 5.

58. "Give Her Great Praise," *Columbus (KS) Daily Advocate,* December 22, 1916, 6.

59. "Majestic Theater," advertisement, *Journal Gazette,* Mattoon, IL, February 14, 1917, 8.

60. "Playing Independent and Getting Business," *Missouri Breeze,* Chicago, IL, January 19, 1917.

61. "Strike of White Rats in Chicago Didn't Materialize," *New York Clipper,* February 14, 1918, 15.

62. "Pickets Busy at Chicago Houses," *New York Clipper,* March 14, 1917, 5.

63. "Cora Corson Issues Booklets," *New York Clipper,* March 14, 1917, 15.

64. "Pickets Busy at Chicago Houses."

65. "Chicago, March 12," *Billboard,* March 17, 1917, 9.

66. "Pickets Busy at Chicago Houses."

67. "More Attempted Strikes by W.R.A.U. Are Fiascos," *Billboard,* March 17, 1917, 6, 8.

68. "Picketing Injunction," *Variety,* March 23, 1917, 6.

69. "Picketers in Blacklist," *Variety,* March 23, 1917, 7.

70. "Agents Will Lose Franchises if Booking Blacklisted Acts," *Variety,* March 23, 1917, 1.

71. "Mountford's Wild Statement Enrages Small Time Acts" and "Mountfordism Dead in Chicago and Boston," Daily Bulletin no. 9, *Variety,* March 10, 1917, 3–4.

72. "Mountfordism Dead in Chicago and Boston."

73. "Chicago, March 19," *Billboard,* March 24, 1917, 190.

74. "Cora Youngblood Corson," *Variety,* March 23, 1917, 9.

75. "Oklahoma Girl Wakes Up 'Chi,'" *Morning Tulsa (OK) Daily World,* April 1, 1917, 11.

76. Segrave, *Actors Organize,* 137.

77. "Theresa Maridol," *New York Clipper,* April 25, 1917, 23.

78. "Spahn Has White Rat Show," *New York Clipper,* April 25, 1917, 5.

79. "Big Vaudeville Program at Apollo Tomorrow," *Bureau County Tribune,* Princeton, IL, April 27, 1917, 1.

80. "All-Star Vaudeville," *Henry (IL) Republican,* May 3, 1917, 1.

81. "8 Big Acts," advertisement, *Rock Island (IL) Argus,* May 12, 1917, 7.

82. "Collinsville," *Tulsa (OK) Democrat,* June 24, 1917, 20; "Mr. and Mrs. Glenn Condon," *Tulsa (OK) Daily World,* August 5, 1917, 20.

83. Letter from Theodore Debs to Cora Youngblood Corson, September 5, 1917, Eugene V. Debs Collection.

84. Telegram from Cora Youngblood Corson to Theodore Debs, October 3, 1917, Eugene V. Debs Collection.

85. "Blacklisted Act Barred from VMPA Theatres," *Variety,* October 19, 1917, 6.

86. "Mountford Admits Rats' Funds Were Place in Realty Stock" and "Fay's Theatre in Bad," *Variety,* November 9, 1917, 7.

87. "Fay's Theatre in Bad,"

88. "Fay Organizing Independents?," *Variety,* November 16, 1917, 6.

89. "Quigley Suggests Deception," *Variety,* November 16, 1917, 6.

5. WAR ABROAD

1. Sellars, "Green Corn Rebellion."

2. Babic, *America's Changing Icons,* 27, 45.

3. Ibid., 1–2, 26.

4. "Keith Circuit in War," *Billboard,* December 28, 1918, 3, 59.

5. Letter from Cora Youngblood Corson to Robert Williams, 20648.15.4, box 1, and photograph of Cora Youngblood Corson, 20648.15.2, box 1, Industries and Occupations, Robert L. Williams Collection.

6. "London Letter," *Billboard,* December 8, 1917, 67. I am unable to ascertain A. Scranton's first name.

7. "Prodigies to Tour England," *New York Clipper,* December 19, 1917, 9.

8. "Condon Goes to Europe," *Billboard,* December 29, 1917, 32.

9. "Cora Youngblood Corson," *Billboard,* December 22, 1917, 36.

10. Journals of Ida Mundell, December 1917–July 1919, unpublished MS, author's collection. Unless otherwise noted, all quotes in this chapter come from these journals.

11. "Webb Gives 'Sidelight' on Condon's Journey," *Daily Oklahoman,* Oklahoma City, March 3, 1918, 25.

12. "Uncle Sam's Nieces in London Unafraid During Bomb Raid," *Waterloo (IA) Evening Courier and Reporter,* May 16, 1918, 8; "Bombs Didn't Scare a Bunch of Pretty Oklahoma Actresses," *Tulsa (OK) Daily World,* May 20, 1918, 7; "U.S. Girls Prevented Panic," *Bristow (OK) Record and the Bristow Enterprise,* May 23, 1918, 3; "German Bombs Fail to Scare the Youngblood-Corson Girls," *American-Democrat,* Anadarko, OK, May 30, 1918, 1; "Hoosier Girls in England Are Quiet During Attack," *Indianapolis (IN) Star,* May 19, 1918, 45.

13. "Girls Are Brave Ones," *Hutchinson (KS) News,* May 15, 1918, 12.

14. "Representative Glenn Condon to Speak Here," *American-Democrat,* Anadarko, OK, April 18, 1918, 1.

15. "Short Locals," *Anadarko (OK) Tribune,* May 30, 1918, 2.

16. "Girls Are Brave Ones."

17. "Making Hit in England," *Billboard,* August 3, 1918, 8.

18. "Cora Youngblood Corson and Her Eight," advertisement, *Musical Truth,* May 1918.

19. Indiana Historical Commission, *Gold Star Honor Roll,* 248.

20. "Touring Ireland," *Billboard,* December 28, 1918, 59.

21. "Oklahoma Music in Staid Old England," *Tulsa (OK) World,* January 26, 1919, 2.

22. "Cora Youngblood Corson," *Billboard,* April 26, 1919, 6.

23. "Corson's Instrumentalists Are Advertising Anadarko," *American-Democrat,* Anadarko, OK, February 13, 1919, 1; "Cora Youngblood Corson Talented Oklahoma Girl Tells an Interesting Story," *Tulsa (OK) Democrat,* June 8, 1919, 15.

24. I am unable to ascertain the first name of Mr. Sullivan.

25. "Cora Youngblood Corson Talented Oklahoma Girl."

26. "Gene Delmont to Box de Pontheiu for K.C.'s Tonight," *Chicago Tribune,* Paris edition, May 9, 1919, 4.

27. "Cora Youngblood Corson Talented Oklahoma Girl."

28. Cornebise, "Der Rhein Entlang," 183.

29. Rudin, *Armistice 1918,* 426.

30. Scanlon, *God Have Mercy on Us!,* 155.

31. "Oklahoma Girl Receives One of the Highest Honors of War," *Tulsa (OK) World,* July 13, 1919, 17.

32. "Gladys Cronk Plays for AEF in Germany," *Montfort (WI) Mail,* July 10, 1919, 1.

33. "Anadarko Girls Entertain U.S. Soldiers in Germany," *American-Democrat,* Anadarko, OK, June 26, 1919, 8.

34. "Oklahoma Girl Receives One of the Highest Honors of War."

35. "Gladys Cronk Plays for AEF in Germany."

36. Gregory, *Story of One Marine,* 240.

37. "Letters to the Editor," *Billboard,* June 21, 1919, 16.

38. "Bon Voyage Troupe Entertains Yanks on Ships in the Harbor," *Pontanezen Duckboard,* Brest, France, July 23, 1919, 3.

39. "Jerome in Booking Business," *Billboard,* October 25, 1919, 6.

40. Gregory, *Story of One Marine,* 241.

41. "Cora Youngblood Corson Instrumentalists," pamphlet, 1919.

42. "Tulsa Woman Played for the Boys 'Over There.'"

43. "K.C. Concert a Success," *Chicago Tribune,* Paris edition, August 6, 1919, 2.

44. "Corson's Instrumentalists Are Advertising Anadarko."

45. "White Rats Chief Sails to Aid Actor Strike," *Chicago (IL) Daily Tribune,* August 14, 1919, 3.

46. Sanjek, *American Popular Music and Its Business,* 21.

47. Slide, *Encyclopedia of Vaudeville,* 368.

6. THE FALL

1. Letter and picture postcard from Cora Youngblood Corson to Governor Robert Williams, February 27, 1919, box 2, folder 14a, record group 8-C-3-2, Governor Robert L. Williams collection, Oklahoma State Archives.

2. Wertheim, *Vaudeville Wars*, 234–36.

3. Kenrick, "Sound + Hollywood = Panic."

4. "Boys Dare Not Brag of Prowess to These Girls," *Cincinnati (OH) Commercial Tribune*, February 1, 1920, 11.

5. "Oklahoma Has Produced Many Theatrical Stars," *Tulsa (OK) Democrat*, September 7, 1919, 42.

6. "K. of C. Octette at Palace Theater," *Hartford (CT) Courant*, September 28, 1919, 29.

7. "K. of C. Octet at Grand," *Evening Public Ledger*, Philadelphia, PA, January 10, 1920, 13.

8. "Cora Youngblood Corson Now in Keith-Booked Theatre," *Variety*, September 19, 1919, 3.

9. Segrave, *Actors Organize*, 140.

10. "Cora Youngblood Corson," *Dramatic Mirror*, December 18, 1919, 1953.

11. "At Poli's," *Evening News*, Wilkes-Barre, PA, November 11, 1919, 2.

12. Bell, "K. of C. Octette," *Variety*, November 28, 1919, 21.

13. "Three-A-Day Policy May Be Adopted by Orpheum Circuit," *Billboard*, December 20, 1919, 35.

14. "I, Cora Youngblood Corson," *Billboard*, December 20, 1919, 51.

15. "Royal," *New York Clipper*, January 7, 1920, 9.

16. "Miss Graycia Acton," *Anadarko (OK) Tribune*, May 20, 1920, 1.

17. "Vaudeville Actors Home," *Variety*, January 31, 1920, 5.

18. "Cora Youngblood Corson . . . ," *Billboard*, March 20, 1920, 46.

19. "The Vaudeville Actors' Haven," *Billboard*, June 5, 1920, 20.

20. "Rest Room Discussed," *Perry (OK) Republican*, July 8, 1920, 1; "Haven for Vaudeville Actors May Be Located in Okla.," *Ponca City (OK) News*, July 9, 1920, 6.

21. "The Vaude. Actor's Haven," *Billboard*, July 31, 1920, 20.

22. "Vaudeville Actors' Haven," August 7, 1920.

23. "Cora Youngblood Corson . . . ," *Oklahoma City (OK) Times*, October 2, 1920, 66.

24. "A GBC Special," *Geary (OK) Times-Journal*, November 18, 1920, 1.

25. "Pie Supper at M.E. Church," *American-Democrat*, Anadarko, OK, December 15, 1920, 1.

26. "Big Dance and AEF Entertainment," advertisement, *Mountain View (OK) Times*, February 11, 1921, 1; "American Legion Dance," advertisement, *Daily Democrat-Chief*, Hobart, OK, February 24, 1921, 2.

27. "Dance," advertisement, *American-Democrat*, Anadarko, OK, March 30, 1921, 5.

28. Letter from Cora to Charles Corson, March 21, 1921, author's collection,

29. "Empress Theater," advertisement, *Springfield (MO) News-Leader*, May 8, 1921, 16.

30. "Times Square Halts to Honor the Dead," *Vaudeville News*, November 18, 1921, 1.

31. "Many Oklahoma Millionaires in New York Colony," *Frederick (OK) Leader*, June 21, 1921, 1.

32. "Oklahoma Club For Metropolis," *Muskogee (OK) Times Democrat*, November 28, 1921, 2.

33. "Sooners in NY Are to Form Club," *Tulsa (OK) Tribune*, June 19, 1921, 21.

34. "Oklahoma Club for Metropolis."

35. "Uncle Joe in Big Company," *Lincoln County Republican*, Chandler, OK, July 7, 1921, 1.

36. "The Oklahoma Society," *New York (NY) Herald*, January 15, 1922, 36.

37. "See Indian Dance," *Oklahoma News*, Oklahoma City, January 21, 1922, 2.

38. "Native Indian Dances," *New York Herald*, January 22, 1922, 34.

39. "Cora Youngblood, Cherokee . . . ," *Pittsburgh (PA) Press*, January 29, 1922.

40. "Guns Boom Today in Echo of '89ers' Run 33 Years Ago," *Muskogee (OK) Daily Phoenix*, April 22, 1922, 1.

41. Bold, "Indigenous Presence in Vaudeville and Early Cinema," 160.

42. "Meeting Was Biggest Event in Sooner-Gotham History," *Morning Tulsa (OK) Daily World*, May 14, 1922, 26.

43. "Leslie Spahn Sued," *Billboard*, December 31, 1921, 14.

44. "Spahn in Bankruptcy," *Billboard*, February 18, 1922, 15.

45. "Miss Cora Youngblood Corson," *Anadarko (OK) Tribune*, November 9, 1922, 5.

46. "County Commissioners Tells SF Kiwanis Club of Road Construction," *Argus-Leader*, Sioux Falls, SD, September 20, 1922, 2.

47. "Cold Is No Bar to Shrine Circus," *Tulsa (OK) World*, November 15, 1922.

48. "With Moore's Indoor Circus," *Billboard*, December 9, 1922, 113.

49. "Four Groups for Radio," *Oregon Daily Journal*, Portland, December 12, 1922, 14.

50. "At Nebraska State Fair," *Brady (NE) Vindicator*, August 16, 1923, 1.

51. "Andrew County Fair Crowd Good," *St. Joseph (MO) Gazette*, August 30, 1923; "Music Draws Large Crowd," *Lincoln (NE) Journal Star*, September 3, 1923, 5.

52. "Fair Board Visits Rotary," *Lincoln (NE) Journal Star*, September 4, 1923, 11.

53. "Fair Records Are Broken," *Nebraska State Journal*, Lincoln, September 4, 1923, 5.

54. "Cora Youngblood Corson Sextet Broadcasts Act," *Billboard*, December 8, 1923, 23.

55. "Family Theater," advertisement, *Democrat and Chronicle*, Rochester, NY, January 11, 1924, 26.

56. "Columbia Burlesque," advertisement, *Billboard*, April 5, 1924, 14.

57. *Giggles* brochure, April 10, 1924, private collection.

58. "Giggles," *Variety*, April 9, 1924, 8.

59. "Playhouse," advertisement, *Passaic (NJ) Daily News*, April 19, 1924, 9; "Broadway Reade's," advertisement, *Daily Record*, Long Branch, NJ, May 7, 1924, 4; "Cora Youngblood Corson," advertisement, *Pottsville (PA) Republican*, May 27, 1924, 4.

60. "Frederick V. Bowers," *York (PA) Daily Record*, June 9, 1924, 7.

61. "Bowers' 'Gang' Closes," *Variety*, July 30, 1924, 5.

62. "Bowers Company Offers Whole Change Last Half," *Evening News*, Harrisburg, PA, June 18, 1924, 20.

63. "At Polis," *Times-Tribune,* Scranton, PA, July 2, 1924, 20.

64. "Palace Today," *Times Herald,* Olean, NY, October 27, 1924, 20.

65. "County Fair Opened at Noon Today," *Times,* Munster, IN, September 16, 1924, 1.

66. "Cora Youngblood Corson Gets Keith Route," *Billboard,* November 29, 1924, 18.

67. Conn promotional postcard, 1924, private collection.

68. "New York Conn Co. Puts Over Excellent Publicity," *Music Trade Review,* December 13, 1924, 111.

69. "The Unwanted, An English Picture Comes to Proctor's," *Yonkers (NY) Statesman,* January 7, 1925, 7.

70. "Ladies Orchestra, Capitol," *New Britain (CT) Daily Herald,* March 19, 1925, 5.

71. "Cora Youngblood Corson," *Morning Call,* Paterson, NJ, April 6, 1925, 12.

72. "Mrs. Youngblood Passes Away After Short Illness," *American-Democrat,* Anadarko, OK, February 11, 1925, 1.

73. "J. M. Youngblood . . . ," *Vaudeville News,* July 7, 1925, 14.

74. "Noted Musical Act Coming to Midland," *Hutchinson (KS) News,* September 12, 1925, 5; "Orpheum," *Daily Oklahoman,* Oklahoma City, September 16, 1925, 5.

75. "Former State School Girl Directs Women's Band," *Oklahoma News,* Oklahoma City, September 17, 1925, 4.

76. "They Appear Here Tonight," *Herald-Press,* St. Joseph, MI, January 30, 1926, 2.

77. "Cora Youngblood Corson . . . ," *News-Palladium,* Benton Harbor, MI, February 1, 1926, 2.

78. "Starting Thursday . . . ," *Messenger-Inquirer,* Owensboro, KY, February 24, 1926, 2.

79. "Vaudeville Bill at Smalley's," *Morning Herald,* advertisement, Johnstown, NY, February 12, 1927, 1.

80. Rowland Field, "The New Play," *Brooklyn (NY) Times Union,* May 11, 1927, 70.

81. J. Brooks Atkinson, "The Play," *New York Times,* May 11, 1927.

82. "Mr. and Mrs. Fred Acton," *American-Democrat,* Anadarko, OK, September 19, 1928, 5.

83. Kessler, *Sins of the Father,* 53.

7. RETIREMENT

1. Troutman, "Joe Shunatona," 18.

2. Deloria, *Indians in Unexpected Places,* 188.

3. Lichtman, *Prejudice and the Old Politics,* 68.

4. Debra Goodrich, "From Teepee to Capitol Dome," *Wild West,* June 2018, 51–53. Goodrich is the Garvey Texas Foundation Historian in Residence at the Fort Wallace Museum and has written a book on Curtis titled *From the Reservation to Washington: The Rise of Charles Curtis.*

5. Troutman, *Indian Blues,* 5.

6. "Indians Send Orchestra to Inauguration," *Hartford (CT) Courant,* February 25, 1929, 21.

7. "Indians Stop in City on Way to Inaugural Ball," *South Bend (IN) Tribune,* February 26, 1929, 14.

8. "Indians Send Orchestra to Inauguration."

9. "Indians Stop in City on Way to Inaugural Ball."

10. E. Ray Goetz and Lou A. Hirsch, "Wildflower," musical score (Shapiro, 1908).

11. "Oompah Squaw," *Daily News,* New York, March 11, 1929, 53; "Oompah Princess," *Standard Union,* Brooklyn, NY, March 12, 1929, 8.

12. "Hoover Inaugural Parade to Be Filmed from Blimps," *News-Press,* Fort Meyers, FL, February 25, 1929, 1.

13. Inaugural Committee, *Official Program: Inaugural Ceremonies.*

14. Troutman, "Joe Shunatona," 21.

15. Powers, "Native American Music," 147.

16. "Indian Chief and Band on Big Air Program," *Morning Call,* Allentown, PA, March 12, 1929, 29.

17. "Radio Programs," advertisement, *Indiana (PA) Gazette,* March 12, 1929, 6.

18. "U.S. Indian Reservation Band Comes to Prospect Theatre," *Brooklyn (NY) Times Union,* March 17, 1929, 65.

19. "Indian Band on WGBI," *Scranton (PA) Republican,* March 30, 1929, 17.

20. "Poli's," advertisement, *Evening News,* Wilkes-Barre, PA, April 4, 1929, 5.

21. Will Abel, "U.S. Indian Reservation Band," *Variety,* March 27, 1929, 41.

22. "Indian Band at the B. F. Keith Memorial," *Boston (MA) Globe,* April 9, 1929, 33.

23. "Indian Band at State House and City Hall," *Boston (MA) Globe,* April 9, 1929, 8.

24. "Indian Musicians Serenade Coolidge," *Boston (MA) Globe,* April 11, 1929, 12.

25. Bige, "Albee," *Variety,* April 17, 1929, 50.

26. "Indians Stop in City on Way to Inaugural Ball."

27. "Indian Band Booked for Palace, Chicago," *Billboard,* April 27, 1929, 12.

28. "Even in their theatrical . . . ," *Cincinnati (OH) Enquirer,* August 11, 1929, 64.

29. "Albee," *Cincinnati (OH) Enquirer,* August 11, 1929, 61.

30. "Cuming County Fair," advertisement, *Beemer (NE) Times,* August 22, 1929, 6.

31. "Official Program," *Bancroft (NE) Blade,* August 22, 1929, 6.

32. *Naturalization Petitions for the United States District and Circuit Courts.*

33. "F. A. Barsanti Rites Pending," *Tulsa (OK) Daily World,* August 24, 1950.

34. Oklahoma, U.S., County Marriage Records, 1890–1995.

35. "Illness Is Fatal for Tulsa Woman," *Tulsa (OK) Daily World,* July 13, 1943.

36. "Two Famous Bands to Vie at Inaugural," *Washington (DC) Post,* February 7, 1933, 16.

37. "Novelties Feature Inaugural Ball," *Philadelphia (PA) Inquirer,* February 26, 1933, 34.

38. "Indians to Inaugural," *Radio News-Guide,* Tulsa, OK, February 11, 1933.

39. "Three Are Appointed," *Evening Star,* Washington, DC, February 3, 1933, 17; "First Lady Guest at Inaugural Ball," *Philadelphia (PA) Inquirer,* March 5, 1933, 12.

40. "Most Spectacular in History," *Evening Star,* Washington, DC, February 7, 1933, 19.

41. "Two Famous Bands to Vie at Inaugural."

42. Harry Ferguson, "Shall it Be Hey-Nonny?" *Cincinnati Enquirer,* February 26, 1933, 17.

43. “Oklahoma Indians and Dancers Fill Program,” *Washington (DC) Post*, February 26, 1933, 6.

44. “Indian Princess Is to Play Tuba at Inaugural,” *Dayton (OH) Daily News*, March 1, 1933, 13.

45. “WRC Broadcasts Reaction of Visitors,” *Evening Star*, Washington, DC, March 3, 1933, 4.

46. “First Lady Guest at Inaugural Ball.”

47. Dorothea J. Lewis, “When in Washington Do as Democrats Do,” *La Crosse (WI) Tribune*, March 6, 1933, 4.

48. “The Sportsman,” *Miami (OK) Daily News-Record*, May 6, 1936.

49. “Musical Quiz,” *Tribune*, Scranton, PA, April 27, 1938.

50. “Show Troupe Is Formed at Tulsa,” *El Reno (OK) Daily Tribune*, March 2, 1943; “Hey, Rube, Inc. Will Play at Glennan General Hospital,” *Okmulgee (OK) Daily Times*, November 3, 1943.

51. “Hey Rube to Celebrate Second Anniversary,” *Gruber Guidon*, Camp Gruber, OK, February 16, 1945.

52. “Tulsa Woman Played for the Boys ‘Over There.’”

53. “Illness Is Fatal for Tulsa Woman.”

54. “F. A. Barsanti Rites Pending.”

55. “Cora Youngblood Corson,” *Billboard*, July 24, 1943, 31.

56. “Illness Is Fatal for Tulsa Woman.”

57. “Cora Youngblood Corson,” *Billboard*, July 24, 1943, 31.

58. “Illness Is Fatal for Tulsa Woman.”

8. LEGACY

1. Kibler, *Rank Ladies*, 191.

2. International Women’s Brass Conference, “Pioneer Award,” https://myiwbc.org/awards.

3. Joanna Ross Hersey, Facebook Messenger interview with author, March 18, 2024.

EPILOGUE

1. “Mrs. Henry Fox,” *Leader Telegram*, Eau Claire, WI, March 4, 1938, 2.

2. “Ruth Wanda Hart Goes to Famous Orchestra,” *Journal and Courier*, Lafayette, IN, September 13, 1926, 3; “Winning Fame in Vaudeville,” *Journal and Courier*, April 14, 1925, 13.

BIBLIOGRAPHY

ARCHIVES

Anadarko Philomathic Museum, Anadarko, Oklahoma

Congressional Record, Congress.gov

Eugene V. Debs Collection, Shadows of the Wabash, ISU Special Collections, Cunningham Memorial Library, Indiana State University, Terre Haute

Governor Robert L. Williams collection, Oklahoma State Archives, Oklahoma Department of Libraries, Oklahoma City

Missouri marriage records, Missouri State Archives, Jefferson City

National Archives and Records Administration, Washington, DC

Oklahoma, U.S., County Marriage Records, 1890–1995, Ancestry.com

Robert L. Williams Collection, Oklahoma History Center, Oklahoma City

BOOKS

Babic, Annessa Ann. *America's Changing Icons: Constructing Patriotic Women from World War I to the Present.* Fairleigh Dickinson University Press, 2018.

Berglund, Jeff, Jan Johnson, and Kimberli Lee. *Indigenous Pop: Native American Music from Jazz to Hip Hop.* University of Arizona Press, 2016.

Berkhofer, Robert F. *The White Man's Indian.* Vintage, 1978.

Bird, S. Elizabeth. *Dressing in Feathers: The Construction of the Indian in American Popular Culture.* Westview Press, 1996.

Bold, Christine. *"Vaudeville Indians" on Global Circuits: 1880s to 1930s.* Yale University Press, 2022.

Browder, Laura. *Slippery Characters: Ethnic Impersonators and American Identities.* University of North Carolina Press, 2000.

Dawkins, Marcia Alesan. *Clearly Invisible: Racial Passing and the Color of Cultural Identity.* Baylor University Press, 2012.

Debo, Angie. *Geronimo: The Man, His Time, His Place.* University of Oklahoma Press, 1996.

Deloria, Philip J. *Indians in Unexpected Places.* University Press of Kansas, 2004.

———. *Playing Indian.* Yale University Press, 1998.

Gerstle, Gary. *American Crucible: Race and Nation in the Twentieth Century.* Princeton University Press, 2001.

Gilbert, James. *Whose Fair? Experience, Memory, and the History of the Great St. Louis Exposition.* University of Chicago Press, 2009.

Goodrich, Debra. *From the Reservation to Washington: The Rise of Charles Curtis.* TwoDot, 2024.

Green, Lucy. *Music, Gender, Education.* Cambridge University Press, 1997.

Gregory, James P., Jr. *The Story of One Marine: The World War I Letters and Photos of Pvt. Thomas L. Stewart.* Hellgate, 2017.

Haupert, Michael J. *The Entertainment Industry.* Greenwood, 2006.

Hauptman, Laurence M., and L. Gordon McLester III. *The Oneida Indians in the Age of Allotment, 1860–1920.* University of Oklahoma Press, 2006.

Huhndorf, Shari M. *Going Native: Indians in the American Cultural Imagination.* Cornell University Press, 2001.

Inaugural Committee. *Official Program: Inaugural Ceremonies.* W. F. Roberts, 1929.

Indiana Historical Commission. *Gold Star Honor Roll: A Record of Indiana Men and Women who Died in the Service of the United States and the Allied Nations in the World War, 1914–1918.* Indiana Historical Commission, 1921.

Kenrick, John. "Sound + Hollywood = Panic." *History of Musical Film—1927–30: Part 2.* musicals101.com, 2004.

Kessler, Ronald. *The Sins of the Father: Joseph P. Kennedy and the Dynasty He Founded.* Warner Books, 1996.

Kibler, M. Alison. *Rank Ladies: Gender and Cultural Hierarchy in American Vaudeville.* University of North Carolina Press, 1999.

La Barre, Weston. *Culture in Context.* Duke University Press, 1980.

Lichtman, Allan J. *Prejudice and the Old Politics: The Presidential Election of 1928.* Lexington Books, 2000.

Naturalization Petitions for the United States District and Circuit Courts, Northern District of Illinois, and Immigration and Naturalization Service District 9, 1840–1950. Microfilm serial M1285, roll 22, National Archives and Records Administration, Washington, DC.

Owens, Louis. *Mixedblood Messages: Literature, Film, Family, Place.* University of Oklahoma Press, 1998.

Parezo, Nancy J., and Don D. Fowler. *Anthropology Goes to the Fair: The 1904 Louisiana Exposition.* University of Nebraska Press, 2007.

Phillips, Katrina. *Staging Indigeneity.* University of North Carolina Press, 2021.

Polito, Robert. *Savage Art: A Biography of Jim Thompson.* Vintage, 1995.

Pratt, Mary Luis. *Imperial Eyes: Travel Writing and Transculturation.* Routledge, 2008.

Quaife, Dorothy Morris. *Jeremiah Youngblood: A Genealogy.* American Press, 1991.

Rudin, Harry R. *Armistice 1918.* Yale University Press, 1944.

Saler, Bethel. *The Settler's Empire: Colonialism and State Formation in America's Old Northwest.* University of Pennsylvania Press, 2015.

Sanjek, Russel. *American Popular Music and Its Business: The First Four Hundred Years,* vol. 3, *From 1900 to 1984.* Oxford University Press, 1988.

Santelli, Robert, Holly George-Warren, and Jim Brown. *American Roots Music.* Harry N. Abrams, 2001.

Scanlon, William T. *God Have Mercy on Us!* Houghton-Mifflin, 1929.

Schwartz, Richard I., and Iris J. Schwartz. *Bands at the St. Louis World's Fair of 1904: Information, Photographs, and Database.* Published by the authors, 2003.

Segrave, Kerry. *Actors Organize: A History of Union Formation Efforts in America, 1880–1919.* McFarland, 2008.

Sexton, Steven Brent. "Imagining Choctaw: Self-Imagination and Settler Colonialism." PhD diss., University of Oklahoma, 2017.

Slide, Anthony. *The Encyclopedia of Vaudeville.* Greenwood Press, 1994.

Smith, Jim. *Republic, Missouri: Home of 3,000 Good Neighbors.* Western Printing Company, 1971.

Stein, Howard F., and Robert F. Hill. *The Culture of Oklahoma.* University of Oklahoma Press, 1993.

Stewart, Travis D. *No Applause—Just Throw Money: The Book That Made Vaudeville Famous.* Faber and Faber, 2005.

Sullivan, Jill, ed. *Women's Bands in America: Performing Music and Gender.* Rowman & Littlefield, 2017.

Trachtenberg, Alan. *Shades of Hiawatha: Staging Indians, Making Americans, 1880–1930.* Hill and Wang, 2004.

Troutman, John W. *Indian Blues: American Indians and the Politics of Music, 1879–1934.* University of Oklahoma Press, 2009.

Veracini, Lorenzo. *Settler Colonialism: A Theoretical Overview.* Palgrave Macmillan, 2010.

Wertheim, Arthur F. *Vaudeville Wars: How the Keith–Albee and Orpheum Circuits Controlled the Big-Time and Its Performers.* Palgrave Macmillan, 2006.

ARTICLES

Bold, Christine. "Indigenous Presence in Vaudeville and Early Cinema." *JCMS Journal of Cinema and Media Studies* 60, no. 2 (Winter 2021): 157–62.

Cornebise, Alfred E. "Der Rhein Entlang: The American Occupation Forces in Germany, 1918–1923, A Photo Essay." *Military Affairs* 46, no. 4 (December 1982): 183.

Cumberledge, Jason P. "Instrument and Gender as Factors in the Perceptions of Musicians and Musical Performance." *Contributions to Music Education* 43 (2018): 159–74.

Hersey, Joanna Ross. "'An Attraction of Unusual Merit': Women's Bands on the Vaudeville Stage." In Sullivan, *Women's Bands in America.*

Howe, Sondra Wieland. "Town Bands, 1880–1920." In Sullivan, *Women's Bands in America.*

Maclead, Beth Abelson. "Whence Comes the Lady Timpanist? Gender and Instrumental Musicians in America, 1853–1990." *Journal of Social History* 27 (Winter 1993): 291–309.

Meyers, Brian D. "Helen May Butler and Her Ladies' Military Band: Being Professional During the Golden Age of Bands." In Sullivan, *Women's Bands in America.*

"The People, The Place: Native Americans in Iowa." February–March 1991. Iowa University Libraries, University of Iowa, https://www.lib.uiowa.edu/exhibits/previous/native.

Pickard, Hanna. "What Is Personality Disorder?" *Philosophy, Psychiatry, & Psychology* 18, no. 3 (September 2011): 181–84.

Platt, Orville H. "Problems in the Indian Territory." *North American Review* 160, no. 459 (February 1895): 195–202.

Powers, William K. "Native American Music." In Santelli et al., *American Roots Music.*

Rice, G. William. "The Mythology of the Oklahoma Indians: A Survey of the Legal Status of Indian Tribes in Oklahoma." *American Indian Law Review* 6, no. 2 (1979): 259–328.

Riffel, Carolyn, and Betty Bell. "Anadarko." In Oklahoma Historical Society, *Encyclopedia of Oklahoma History and Culture,* https://www.okhistory.org/publications/enc/entry.php?entry=AN002.

Scherer, Anita. "Top Brass." *American Music Teacher* 49, no. 6 (June/July 2000): 63.

Sellars, Nigel Anthony. "Green Corn Rebellion." In Oklahoma Historical Society, *Encyclopedia of Oklahoma History and Culture,* https://www.okhistory.org/publications/enc/entry?entry=GR022.

Troutman, John. "Joe Shunatona and the United States Indian Reservation Orchestra." In Berglund et al., *Indigenous Pop.*
Wolfe, Patrick. "Settler Colonialism and the Elimination of the Native." *Journal of Genocide Research* 8, no. 4, (December 2006): 387–409.

MAGAZINES

Billboard
Music Trade Review
The Performer
The Player
The Standard and Vanity Fair
Variety
Wild West

NEWSPAPERS

For this work, I consulted 195 newspapers from the period 1901 to 1943, from cities throughout the United States. Details of each can be found in the endnotes.

INDEX

Page numbers in italics refer to figures.

www.ingramcontent.com/pod-product-compliance
Lightning Source LLC
LaVergne TN
LVHW091147080826
845145LV00008B/2287
* 9 7 8 0 8 0 7 1 8 6 7 7 0 *